Edwin Tunis

Tunis's topographical and pictorial guide to Niagara Falls and route book to Montreal

Edwin Tunis

Tunis's topographical and pictorial guide to Niagara Falls and route book to Montreal

ISBN/EAN: 9783337147655

Printed in Europe, USA, Canada, Australia, Japan

Cover: Foto ©Andreas Hilbeck / pixelio.de

More available books at **www.hansebooks.com**

Fouquet's Hotel,

PLATTSBURGH, N. Y.

This Hotel is situated at Plattsburgh, upon the western shore of Lake Champlain, on the banks of Cumberland Bay, which was the scene of the naval battle of 1814. Fine views can be had from its piazzas in all directions, which include the Lake, the Islands, the Green Mountains on the east, the Adirondacks on the south, presenting every variety of scenery—the wild, the picturesque, the grand. This Hotel is retired, it has beautiful garden and flower grounds, purest of spring water, spacious and well ventilated rooms, which, together with the pleasant drives in the vicinity, offer attractions to the seeker after health and pleasure that cannot be surpassed.

To See Lake Champlain and Lake George by Daylight.

Leave Montreal by the Afternoon Train, and arrive at Fouquet's Hotel to supper. Take Day Boat the following day for Whitehall or Lake George. Arrive at Saratoga via Whitehall to supper.

For Lake George.

Leave the steamer at Ticonderoga, thence by stage four miles around the rapids to Lake George, thence by Steamer MINNE-HA-HA to Caldwell, at the upper end of the Lake, at which place are the ruins of Fort William Henry, of revolutionary fame.

By this arrangement, the Tourist has the advantage of passing, by daylight, through the entire length of two of the noted sheets of water in America, seeing all their varied beauty and portions connected with them, both historical and romantic.

New Route to the Adirondacks.

The Whitehall & Plattsburgh Railroad is now completed and being opened from Plattsburgh to Ausable River Station, a distance of 20 miles, connecting with a four-horse line of stages, running DAILY, to the Principal Summer Resorts of the GREAT WILDERNESS. Tickets for the route can be procured at the principal ticket offices, on the Lake Champlain steamers, and at this hotel.

SEA BATHING
CACOUNA.

St. Lawrence Hall.

The Proprietor begs to inform the Traveling Public that the above First Class Hotel will be opened for the season, about the middle of June.

During the past year it has been thoroughly renovated and improved, and an additional wing has been built, containing twenty family bed rooms, enabling the Hotel to entertain comfortably two hundred and fifty guests, thus affording ample accommodations for the great number that annually flock to this favorite sea-side resort.

He has constructed six Private Bath Rooms in the House, where Invalids and others may have the advantage of Warm or Cold Water Baths at any hour of the day. This improvement has been made at the suggestion of several eminent medical men.

The Grounds have been entirely remodeled. In the rear is an excellent Lawn and Croquet Ground, with Arbors and Summer Houses.

☞ Fishing and Pleasure Boats always on hand.

Rates of Charge:

Transient Visitors, by the Day, ... $2 00
One Week and Over, per Day, ... 1 50

A Liberal Reduction will be made for Families or Individuals wishing to board by the month or for the season.

☞ Telegraph Station for all parts of Canada and the United States, in the office of the Hotel.

☞ CACOUNA can be reached twice daily by Cars from Quebec, and by Steamboat direct from Montreal, four times per week.

Russell's St. Louis Hotel,
ST. LOUIS STREET, QUEBEC.

THE PROPRIETOR of the above first class Establishment begs to draw the attention of Tourists to the comfort and advantages to be found therein.

The ST. LOUIS HOTEL, St. Louis Street, which is unrivaled for size, style and locality in Quebec, is open during the year. It is eligibly situated, near to and surrounded by the most delightful and fashionable promenades, the Governor's Garden, the Citadel, the Esplanade, the Place d'Arms, Durham Terrace, and the Ramparts, from all of which splendid views of the magnificent scenery for which Quebec is so justly celebrated, and which is unsurpassed in any part of the world, can be had.

The Proprietor, in returning thanks for the very liberal patronage he has hitherto enjoyed, informs the public that this Hotel has been thoroughly renovated and embellished, and can now accommodate about 500 visitors; and having also facilities at command to accommodate, without exception, all classes of Tourists, Pleasure Seekers, and the Traveling Public in general, assures them that nothing will be spared on his part that will conduce to the comfort and enjoyment of his guests.

WILLIS RUSSELL, Proprietor.

Alpine House,

GORHAM, N H.

— AND —

Tip Top and Summitt Houses

MOUNT WASHINGTON.

Carriages always in readiness at the Alpine House to convey Passengers to the Tip-Top and Summitt Houses, on Mount Washington, and return same day or remain over night.

J. R. HITCHCOCK, Proprietor.

"AMERICAN"
BOSTON, MASS.

L. RICE & SON,
PROPRIETORS.

Largest First Class Hotel in the City

CENTRALLY LOCATED,

Convenient to Railway Offices and Places of Amusement, and containing

SUITS and SINGLE APARTMENTS

With Bathing and Water Conveniences adjoining.

TUFT'S IMPROVED VERTICAL RAILWAY

Billiard Halls,

TELEGRAPH OFFICE, AND CAFE.

ST. JAMES HOTEL,

MONTREAL.

The undersigned beg to notify the Public that they have purchased the above well known First Class Hotel, which is now carried on as a

Branch Establishment of the St. Lawrence Hall,

Under the management of Mr. SAMUEL MONTGOMERY, (nephew of Mr. Hogan), and Mr. FREDERICK GERIKEN, both well known to the traveling community in the United States and Canada, as being connected with the St. Lawrence Hall.

The St. James is very favorably situated, facing Victoria Square,

IN THE VERY CENTRE OF THE CITY,
And Contiguous to the Postoffice and the Banks.

Its convenience for Business Men is everything that can be desired, as it is in the

Immediate Vicinity of the Wholesale Houses.

The Rooms, being well appointed and ventilated, are cheerful for Families, while the menage will always be unexceptionable, and no pains spared in ministering to the comfort of guests.

The proprietors having leased the adjoining premises, are prepared to offer every inducement to the

SPRING AND FALL TRADE,

And as their Tariff is unexceptionably reasonable, they hope to obtain a large share of public patronage.

H. HOGAN & CO.

St. Lawrence Hall,

Situated on St James Street, MONTREAL.

H. HOGAN, Proprietor.

This First Class Hotel, the largest in Montreal, is situated on St. James street, in the immediate vicinity of the French Cathedral, or Church "Ville Marie," Notre Dame street, adjacent to the Postoffice, Place D'Armes, and Banks; is only one minutes' walk from Grey or Black Nunneries, New Court House, Reading Rooms, "Champ de Mars," where the troops are reviewed, Mechanics' Institute, Bonsecours Market, and the fashionable Stores.

The new Theatre Royal is directly in rear of the House, and several of the best boxes are regularly kept for guests of this Hotel.

The St. Lawrence Hall has long been regarded as the

𝕸ost 𝕻opular and 𝕱ashionable 𝕳otel in 𝕸ontreal,

And is patronized by Government on public occasions, including that of the visit of

H. R. H. THE PRINCE OF WALES AND SUITE, AND THAT OF HIS EXCELLENCY THE GOVERNOR GENERAL AND SUITE.

During the past winter the Hotel has been considerably enlarged, so that in future the proprietor hopes to be able to accommodate comfortably all who may favor him with their patronage.

All Rooms lighted by Gas.

The Consulate Office of the United States is in the Hotel, as well as a Telegraph Office to all parts.

The proprietor begs to announce that, having recently purchased the St. Lawrence Hall property, it is his intention next Fall to pull down and rebuild, with all the modern improvements, including an Elevator, thus making this Hotel second to none in the United States.

Montreal, April, 1871.

SPENCER HOUSE,

NIAGARA FALLS,

American Side.

This House has been planned and built especially for Light, Air and Comfort. Nowhere will the Tourist have a better opportunity to feel at home than at this new Hotel. It is fitted up in the most modern style, with hot and cold Baths, Billiard Rooms, Gas, etc.

It is centrally situated, and within five minutes' walk of the Falls and new Suspension Bridge.

A. CLUCK, Proprietor.

J. B. FOWLER,

Importer of

DIAMONDS,

Fine Gold Watches, Rich Jewelry

RARE GEMS, &c.

ONTARIO STREET, ST. CATHERINES.

N. B.—St. Catherines now outrivals any city in Canada for high class goods, which, together with the celebrated Mineral Springs, are attracting the notice of almost every Traveler.

JAMES D. TAIT,
St. Catherines, Canada,
IMPORTER OF

RICH FRENCH SILKS,

Moire Antiques,   Lyons Velvets,
Irish Poplins,   Thread Laces,

LAMA & REAL LACE SHAWLS,

Sash, Ribbons, French Fans, and

PARIS FANCY ARTICLES,

Courvoissier, Jugla, Alexandres, and Harris

Kid Gloves,

Cotton, Lisle Thread, Silk and Balbriggan
HOSIERY,

GENTS' ENGLISH AND FRENCH FURNISHING GOODS,

FURS,

Manufactured on the premises. Russian and Hudson Bay Sable, Canadian Mink, Royal, Ermine, and South Sea Seal setts of Furs.

☞ South Sea Seal, Astrachan and Royal Ermine Jackets for Ladies.

☞ Mantles, Dresses and Suits made up in Paris and New York style, and on short notice, for convenience of travelers.

CARD.— As St. Catherines is only twenty minutes' trip from the Falls, Tourists should not fail to pay a visit to the celebrated Mineral Springs and to this establishment, as nowhere out of New York are higher classes of imported goods on exposition.   JAMES D. TAIT.

Union Forwarding & Railway Co.

ROYAL MAIL LINE.

Upper Iowa Route,

From OTTAWA to DES JOACHIN RAPIDS, PEMBROKE,

AND ALL INTERMEDIATE PLACES,

Connecting at Sand Point with BROCKVILLE & OTTAWA RAILROAD.

The Line is composed of the following First Class Steamers, commanded by experienced and attentive officers:

"Ann Sisson,"   "Pembroke,"   "Calumet,"
"Alliance,"   "Snow Bird,"   "Pontiac,"
"Jason Gould,"   "Oregon,"   "Emerald."

One of the above Steamers leaves AYLMER every morning (Sundays excepted), at 7.30 A.M., passing through the following Picturesque Lakes by daylight·

DU CHESORA, CHATTS' ISLAND, AND ALLUMEKE.

☞ Especial attention paid to Excursion Parties and Tourists. Visitors to the Capital should not fail to make

The above Delightful Trip.

Descriptive Books can be had on application to

E. BARBER, Niagara Falls.

☞ For further information apply at Office in Ottawa or Aylmer.

R. S. CASSELLS, President.

The Ottawa River Navigation Co's
Mail Steamers,

Queen Victoria,	Prince of Wales,
Capt. H. W. SHEPHERD.	Capt. A. BOWIE.

OFFICE, 10 BONAVENTURA ST., MONTREAL.

Train leaves St. Bonaventura Street Depot, Montreal, every morning (Sundays excepted), at 7.00 A. M., connecting at Lachine with Steamer PRINCE OF WALES, for Carillon; then by Railway to Penoille, connecting with Steamer QUEEN VICTORIA, for Ottawa City, at 6.00 P.M.
Steamer QUEEN VICTORIA leaves Ottawa at 6.30 A.M., Passengers arriving at Montreal at 4.45 A.M.

Tourists will find this a Delightful Trip.

PARCELS EXPRESS DAILY.
☞ BAGGAGE CHECKED THROUGH.

Further information and Tickets can be had at the Railway Depot, at the Office, or on board the Steamers.

R. W. SHEPHERD, President

RICHELIEU COMPANY'S
DAILY ROYAL
Mail  Line
OF STEAMERS
BETWEEN
Montreal and Quebec.

The New and Splendid Iron Steamers

Montreal | *Quebec,*
Capt. NELSON, | Capt. LABELLE,

Leave Montreal and Quebec Daily (Sundays excepted), Every Evening, according to Passengers

A DELIGHTFUL TRIP

Between these two places of interest, to all Tourists in Canada, stopping at Sorrel, Three Rivers and Batiscan.

☞ For further information apply at the Office,

No. 203 Commissioner's Street,

MONTREAL.

J. B. LAMERE, General Manager.

THE NEW AND SPLENDID STEAMER

CITY OF TORONTO
Captain D. MILLOY,
Now Running Daily
BETWEEN
LEWISTON AND TORONTO

Connecting at Toronto Daily at 2 o'clock P.M. with Royal Mail Steamers for Kingston, Montreal, and intermediate ports; also with Express Trains on the Grand Trunk, Great Western and Northern Railroads for all points in Canada, East, West and North. Trains by the New York Central Railroad leave Buffalo at 9 A.M., Niagara Falls at 10 A.M., for Lewiston Daily (Sundays excepted), for Toronto, by Steamer "City of Toronto."

Quickest & Cheapest Route
FROM BUFFALO TO TORONTO.

BE SURE AND ASK FOR TICKETS VIA LEWISTON.

THROUGH TICKETS can be purchased at the Erie St. Depot, Buffalo; No. 1 International Hotel, Niagara Falls, and at the principal Ticket Offices in the United States.

N. MILLOY, AGENT,
No. 8 Front Street, TORONTO.

SEASON 1871.

St. Lawrence & Ottawa Railway

FROM PRESCOTT,

Opposite the City of Ogdensburg, on the River St. Lawrence,

TO THE CITY OF OTTAWA,

The Capital & Seat of Government of the Dominion of Canada.

The attention of Tourists is respectfully invited to this route to and from the City of Ottawa. Trains are run in connection with those of the Grand Trunk Railway, and with the steamers of the Royal Mail Company. On arrival at Prescott or Ogdensburg the Tourist can leave the Steamer or the Railway, and proceed thence by the St. Lawrence & Ottawa Railway, a distance of 54 miles, to the City of Ottawa, where the magnificent Parliamentary Buildings, the Falls of the Chaudiere, spanned by an elegant Suspension Bridge, the extensive Lumbering and other Mills, the celebrated Timber Slides, and the Military Canal Works, surrounded by scenery of unusual grandeur, form a combination of attractions rarely surpassed.

Tickets from Prescott to Ottawa and back, and all information respecting trains, can be obtained from the Pursers on board the Royal Mail Line of Steamers, and from

E. BARBER, No. 1 International Hotel Block,

NIAGARA FALLS.

NOTICE AS TO FREIGHT. Shippers are informed that a Change-Guage Car Pit has been provided at Prescott Junction Freight Shed, by means of which Grain and other Freight loaded on Change-Guage Cars, can come through to Ottawa, without transhipment, thereby ensuring safety and despatch. A Floating Elevator has also been placed at Prescott Wharf, for the convenience of transhipping Grain for Ottawa, from vessels to the Company's cars, during navigation.

THOS. REYNOLDS, Managing Director.

OTTAWA.

B. LUTTRELL, Superintendent.

PRESCOTT.

II

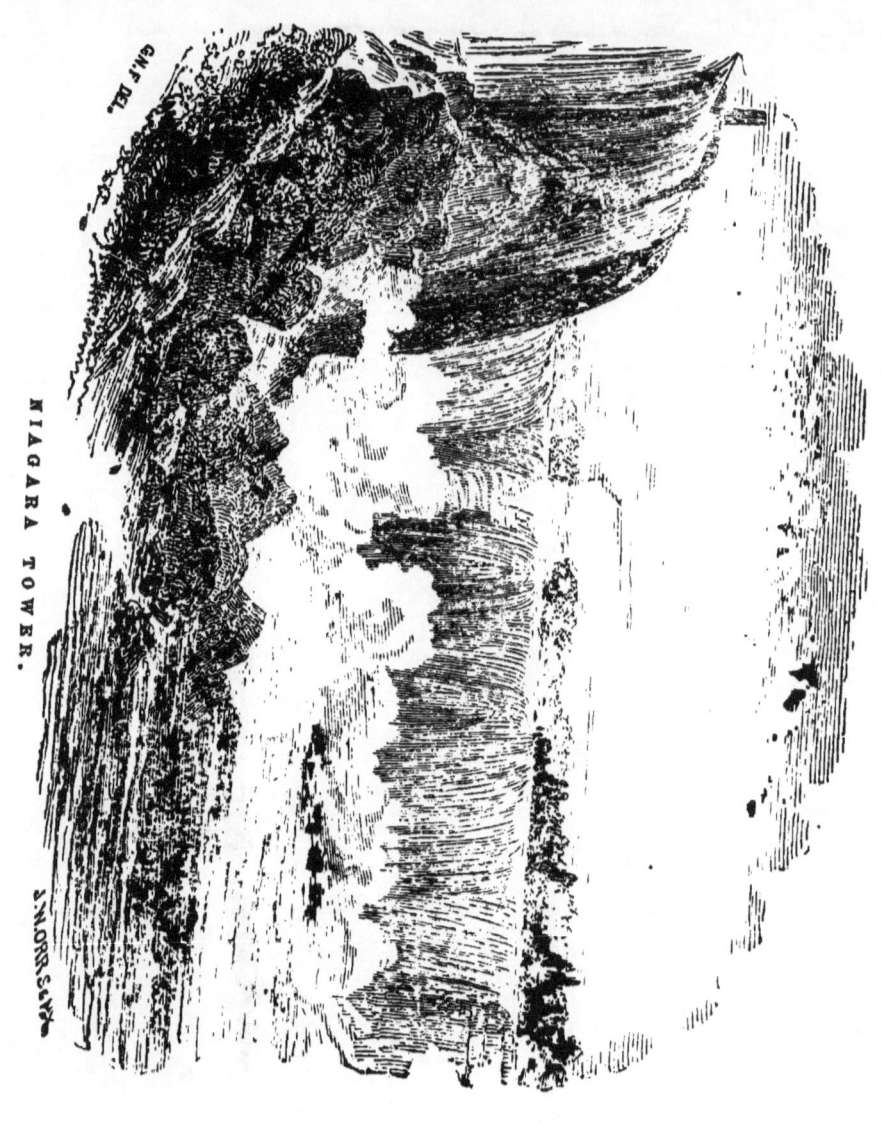

TUNIS'S

TOPOGRAPHICAL AND PICTORIAL

GUIDE

TO

NIAGARA FALLS

AND

ROUTE BOOK TO

Montreal, Quebec, Saratoga, and the
White Mountains;

ALSO,

DESCRIPTION OF THE ST. LAWRENCE, OTTAWA, AND
SAGUENAY RIVERS.

Russell House,

DETROIT, MICH.

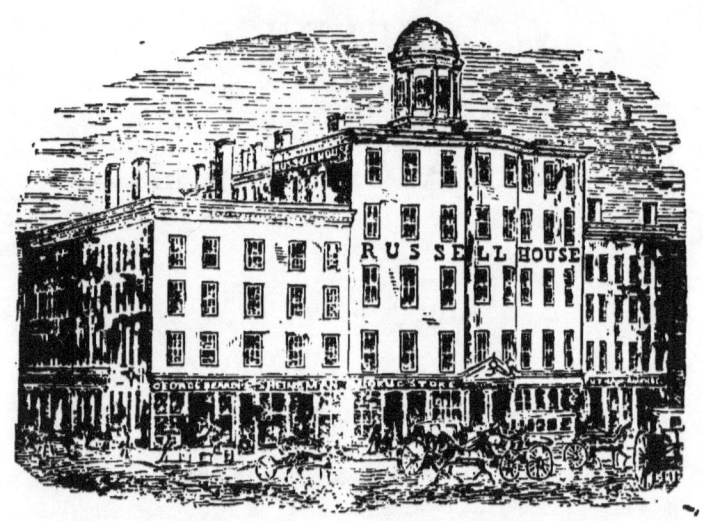

Situated in the most Central part of the City, and facing new City Hall and Opera House.

WITBECK & CHITTENDEN,
Proprietors.

ST. CATHARINES.

Ontario, Canada,

The great Canada Mineral Springs Watering Place, situated twelve miles from Niagara Falls, easily accessible by Great Western Railway.

Stephenson House,

STIMSON & FOWLER, Proprietors.

The original celebrated Artesian Well of Saline Mineral Water, with Baths, is in connection with this first class Hotel, which will be opened on

Monday, May 20, 1872, under new auspices.

The proprietors have at great expense Refitted, Renovated, Papered, and Furnished the Stephenson House for 1872, making it one of the most attractive, pleasant and health preserving places on this continent.

ST. CATHERINES also possesses the rare advantages of city and country combined. Shady walks, delightful drives, fine roads leading to many places of noted interest, which may be found described in the guide, making up for the pleasure seeker or invalid, just those requirements so much sought after, and so seldom found combined in any place as at St. Catherines, the truly celebrated watering place of Canada.

THE MINERAL WATERS

Of ST. CATHERINES Artesian Well (600 feet deep) resemble some of the more celebrated spas in Germany, and excelling any other mineral waters in America.

Pamphlets and Circulars with analysis mailed on application.

Great Central Route!

THE DIRECT & POPULAR ROUTE
—— TO ——

CHICAGO,

And all Points West Southwest and Northwest,

—— IS BY THE ——

MICHIGAN CENTRAL
RAILROAD.

Four Express Trains Daily

To Chicago (except Sunday), and on Sunday a Night Train.

Pullman's Palace Sleeping and Drawing Room Cars on all Night Trains, Ladies' Cars and Luxurious Smoking Cars on all Day Trains.

All coaches of this Road have 6-wheeled Trucks, and possess all modern improvements conducing to health and safety.

FARE AS LOW AS BY ANY OTHER RAILROAD.

C. H. HURD,		**H. E. SARGENT,**
Asst Gen. Supt.,		Gen Supt.,
DETROIT.	[May, 1872.]	CHICAGO.

TOURISTS AND PLEASURE SEEKERS!

1872. 1872.

Summer Arrangement
—OF THE—

Lake Champlain and Lake George
STEAMERS.

The Fashionable Thoroughfare and Pleasure Route
—BETWEEN—

Niagara Falls, Montreal and Lake George,
Saratoga, Troy, Albany, New York,
Mt. Mansfield, The Adirondac
Sporting Grounds, and all

SOUTHERN AND WESTERN POINTS.

2 DAILY TRAINS leave Montreal, connecting at ROUSES POINT with the Elegant and Commodious Steamers.

VERMONT, Capt. W. H. Flagg.
    ADIRONDAC, Capt. Wm. Anderson.
        UNITED STATES, Capt. George Rushlow.
            MONTREAL Capt. Robert J. White.

Forming two daily lines each way through the Lake, connecting at Ticonderoga with Steamer "Minne-ha-ha," through Lake George, and at Whitehall with Trains of Rensselaer and Saratoga Railroad, for Saratoga, Troy, Albany, New York, and all Southern and Western Points.

The Only Route to Lake George, and Only Direct Route to Saratoga.

Through Tickets and Information can be obtained at the Ticket Offices, at Niagara Falls, at the Company's Office, J. N. Bockus, Agent, 59 Great St James Street Montreal, (adjoining St. Lawrence Hall), at the Offices of the Grand Trunk Railway, on board of Steamers, and at the General Office of the Company, Burlington Vt.

May, 1872.   A L INMAN, Gen'l Supt.

THE NEW NORTHWESTERN ROUTE

Detroit, Lansing and Lake Michigan Railroad

THE SHORTEST AND ONLY DIRECT ROUTE

— TO —

LANSING

THE CAPITOL OF THE STATE.

Two Express Trains Daily!

Making Close Connections

At LANSING—with the Jackson, Lansing and Saginaw R. R., for points in the Saginaw Valley;

At IONIA—with Detroit and Milwaukee R. R., for Grand Rapids, Muskegon, etc.

At HOWARD CITY—with Grand Rapids and Indiana R. for Big Rapids and all points in Northern Michigan.

☞ Close Connection made ☜

At DETROIT—with the Great Western Railway of Canada, for Buffalo, Rochester, Boston, New York, Philadelphia, Toronto; and with Grand Trunk Railway, for Montreal, Quebec; and with Cleveland and Lake Superior Lines of Steamers.

A. H. REESE, Supt.

Ladies and Gents Fine Furs
OF EVERY DESCRIPTION,
Manufactured from the Choicest Mink, S S. Seal, Russian and Hudson Bay Skins, always on hand.

W. E. TUNIS,
86 Woodward Ave., Detroit,
WHOLESALE DEALER IN
Books, Stationery
AND PERIODICALS.

Any Book or Paper published, or any article of Stationery, will be sent, prepaid, at regular retail price, to any part of the country.

Howard House,

KINGSTON,

ONTARIO, CANADA.

—[::]—

Captain Swales. - Proprietor.

—[::]—

This first class hotel is centrally located and so arranged as to give guests the greatest amount of comfort.

CONNECTICUT AND PASSUMPSIC RIVERS
—AND—
MOSSAWAIPPI VALLEY R. R.
—RUNNING BETWEEN—

White River Junction and Lennoxville.

Connecting at the former place with Grand Trunk Railroad to Montreal and Quebec, at White River Junction with Vermont Central for Boston, Concord, Manchester, Lawrence, Lowell, Nassau, Salem, &c.,with Connecticut River Railroad for New York and Intermediate Places, as Bellows Falls, South Vernon, Granfield, Springfield, Hartford, &c., &c.

This is the direct and most accessible Route to White Mountains and Franconia, Lake Memphremagog and Willoughby, Quebec and Surrounding Country.

PULLMAN'S
PALACE AND SLEEPING CARS

On all Express Trains connecting with Quebec and Montreal Line, also with lines to New York and Boston.

Passengers by this Route can ascend Mount Washington by Steam Railway. Successfully Operated last year.

Tickets and any information can be obtained of

GUSTAVE LEVE, Agent,
Opposite St. Louis Hotel, Quebec,
Or, WM. CLARK, Agent,
87 Washington St., Boston, Mass.

"AMERICAN,"

Boston, Mass.

L. RICE & SON,
PROPRIETORS.

Largest First Class Hotel in the City!

CENTRALLY LOCATED,

Convenient to Railway Offices and Places of Amusement, and containing

SUITS and SINGLE APARTMENTS,

With Bathing and Water Conveniences adjoining.

Tuft's Improved Vertical Railway,

BILLIARD HALLS,

TELEGRAPH OFFICE, AND CAFE.

PREFACE.

The design of the present work is to supply a lack which a comparison with other works of the kind will best evince.

No other Guide now before the public is either sufficiently recent or sufficiently comprehensive to be safely followed by the tourist, at Niagara, and to the West and North. It is not without confidence, therefore, that we commit this compilation as a reliable and needed "vade mecum" to the traveling public.

IRON BRIDGE TO GOAT ISLAND.

DRY GOODS.

WM. ARTHURS & CO.

25 King Street East,

TORONTO,

IMPORTERS OF BRITISH AND FOREIGN

Dry Goods,

Silks, Satins,   Moire Antiques,
    Irish Poplins,   Fancy Dress Goods,
Real Lyons Mantle Velvets.

THE LARGEST STOCK IN THE DOMINION

Of Alexandres, Josephine and Jouvin's

KID GLOVES,

Also, Dent's Lined Gloves and Mitts, Silk, Merino, Thread and Wool Hosiery, Shirts, Collars, Cuffs, Scarfs, Ties, Braces, Silk and Lawn Handkerchiefs,

—ALSO—

House Furnishing and General Staple Goods.

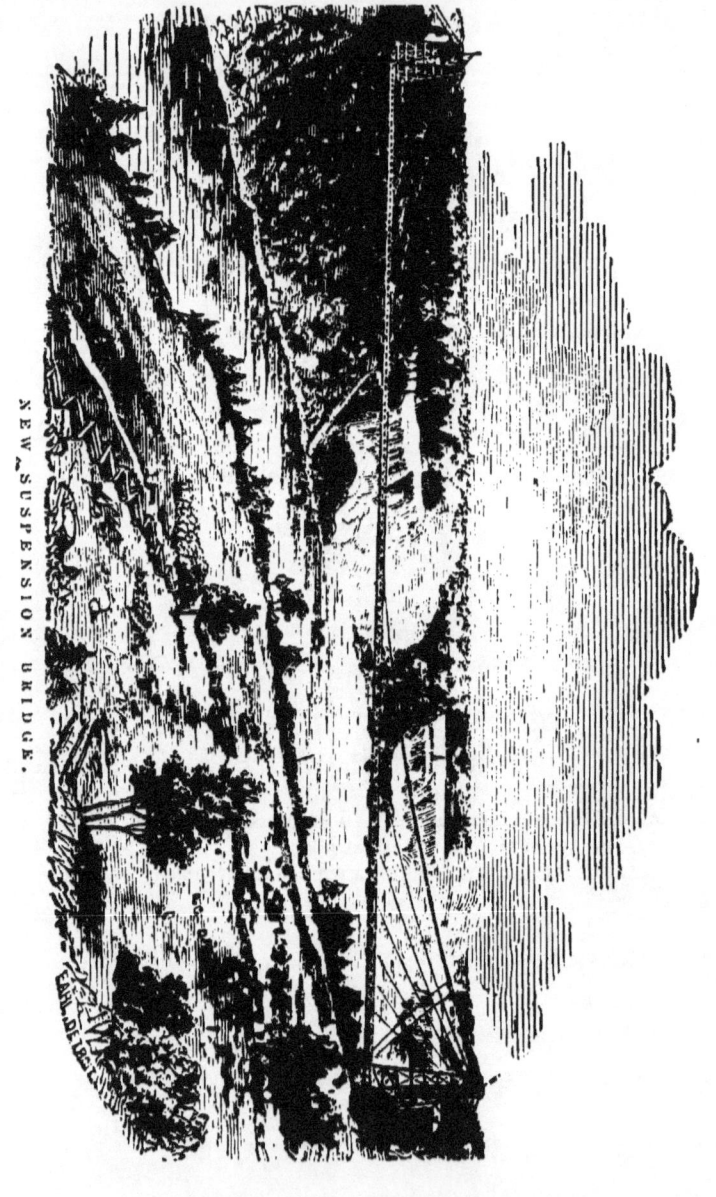

THE ROSSIN HOUSE

TORONTO,
ONTARIO,   CANADA.

Opened August 1, 1867.

Finished with every regard to Comfort and Luxury, and furnished with all

MODERN IMPROVEMENTS,

And will be kept in every way as a First Class Hotel.

G. P. SHEARS, Lessee and Manager.

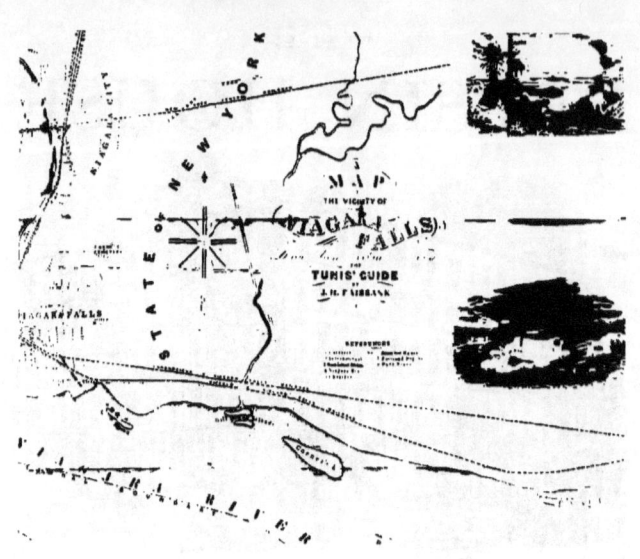

TUNIS'S

GUIDE TO NIAGARA.

Arrival at the Falls.

FROM whatever point of the village you may be starting, a cloud of spray, or the noise of the cataract, will indicate the general direction of your foot-steps. Arriving on Main Street, pass down the street leading between the Cataract and International Hotels, and you are in full view of the river at the point where it is spanned by

Goat Island Bridge.

The old wooden bridge which had stood since 1818 was replaced, by this costly and beautiful structure, in the summer of 1856. The foundations consist of massive oak timber cribs, filled with stone and covered with plates of iron. The superstructure is of iron, and consists of four arches, of ninety feet span each, supported between the abutments of these piers. The whole length of the bridge is, therefore, 360 feet, and its whole width is 27 feet. Of this width a double carriage-way occupies 16¼ feet, and two foot-ways, one on either side of the carriage-way, occupy, each, 5¼ additional feet.

No point commands so fine a view of the rapids as this bridge. The delicate tints of the water are here, especially, enticeable. The waves are breaking constantly into new forms, in each successive change catching the sunlight under new conditions, and throwing it back in some novel transfusion of hues.

It was while the old bridge was repairing, in the summer of 1839, that one of the workmen, a Mr. Chapin, was accidentally thrown from the frame-work into the river, and carried by the current to the first of the two smallest islands below, since called, from this circumstance, Chapin Island. He was thence rescued by the strong nerve and skillful hand of Mr. Joel R. Robinson, a name associated with many a gallant rescue from these waters.

The fall of the river's bed, from the head of the rapids to the verge of the precipice, is 58 feet. This gradual descent, by confusing the lines of vision as you gaze up the river, gives the farthest crest of the rapids a vague and skyish cast, suggestive of the Infinite; so that, turning from this to where the river disappears in its final leap, you seem to have realized in space the similitudes of life

"—— Standing 'twixt two eternities."

Before crossing the bridge, you are at the toll-gate to

GUIDE TO NIAGARA FALLS. 11

Bath Island — Lover's Retreat — Brig Island — Goat Island.

Goat Island Bridge,

(*see page nine,*) leading to the Islands. Fifty cents entitles you for the day, and one dollar for the year, to pass on all of them. The first you reach is Bath Island. Looking up the Rapids, that small, sentimental-looking island on your left is called "Lover's Retreat;" the island just beyond that, Brig Island. That large building on your right is a paper-mill, said to be the largest in the state. Passing from Bath Island over a short bridge, you stand on

Goat Island.

This, though not the largest, is by far the most beautiful island in the Niagara. Long before it was bridged to the American shore, it was visited from time to time by the few to whom its attractions were of more potent consideration than the peril of reaching it. The late Judge Porter, who visited it in 1805, remembered having seen the names of strangers cut into the bark of a beech near Horseshoe Fall, with the subjoined dates of 1771, 1772, and 1779.

The island is now owned by the Porter family, to whom it was ceded by the state of New York in 1818. It derived its name from the circumstance of a Mr. Stedman, of Schlosser, having placed some goats on it to pasture. This was in 1770. The area of the island is sixty-one and a half acres; its circumference about one mile.

Three paths branch off from the road by which you

ascend the bank, the middle one dividing the island into two nearly equal parts, the left leading to the head of the island, and the right (the one usually taken) to the American Fall. Following this path, you are conducted through a colonnade of forest trees, with the rapids at your right, over a space of eighty rods, to the north-western point of the island, called, by what process of association no mortal can tell,

Hog's Back.

It was while walking directly under this point that the lamented Dr. Hungerford, of West Troy, N. Y., was killed in the spring of 1839, by the crumbling of a portion of the rock from above. This is the only accident that has ever occurred at the Falls by the falling of rock.

Passing by a narrow foot-path down the bank, and crossing the short bridge at your right, you stand upon a lovely spot called

Luna Island.

On the northern edge of this island, a few feet above the precipice, is a spot of mournful memory. On June 21, 1849, the family of Mr. Deforest, of Buffalo, together with Mr. Charles Addington, their friend, were viewing the scenery from this point. The party, in fine spirits, were about leaving the island when Mr. Addington, advancing playfully to Miss Annette, the little daughter of Mrs. Deforrest, said, "I am going to throw you in," at the same time lifting her lightly over the edge of the water. With a sudden impulse of fear, the startled child flung herself from his hands, and struck the wild current of the river. With a shriek the young man sprang to her recovery, but before the stricken group on shore had time to speak or move, they had both passed over the precipice. The crushed remains of the lately blooming and buoyant child were found in the afternoon of the same day in the Cave of the Winds; and a few days afterward the body of the gallant but fated young Addington was likewise recovered, and committed with many tears to the village cemetery. This is perhaps the most touching casualty that has ever occurred at the Falls.

Leaving Luna Island, pause for a moment at the foot of the path before you ascend, while we point you out an appearance which certain imaginative persons have been pleased to call

The Three Profiles.

These so called profiles are formed by the inequality of projection in that portion of the precipice which is formed by the western side of Luna Island. The rock is adjacent to, and almost under the American Fall.

The Center Fall.

This is that portion of the American Fall which is cut off by Luna Island. Having now ascended the bank, and rested from your fatigue, pass on a few rods to where a guide-board points out

Cave of the Winds.

Here you will see has been erected a suitable building for the accommodation of visitors wishing to pass under the center fall, and into the Cave of the Winds, a feat which every one, ladies as well as gentlemen, should perform, for probably nowhere about Niagara is grandeur so admirably displayed. New dresses, clean and dry, are at the service of all visitors. For a small fee, an experienced guide will accompany parties under the sheet, and describe in a few words the celebrated leap of Sam. Patch; death of Dr. Hungerford; the recovery of the remains of the ill-fated Miss DeForest and Charles Addington, and many other incidents connected with this particular locality, better than we could in many pages.

Whirlpool Rapids and Double Elevator.

At this point an elevator has been built, worked by a water wheel some 300 feet below the top of the bank, enabling the visitor to reach the water's edge without fatigue.

Here bursts upon the view one of the most beautiful and sublime sights to be seen at Niagara.

Through the narrow gorge rush all the waters of the Upper Lakes.

The immense under current forces the water in the center of the stream, and 20 or 40 feet above the outer edges of the river.

There is probably no place in the vicinity of Niagara more to be admired by the visitor than this romantic spot.

The New Suspension Bridge at Niagara Falls.

The New Suspension Bridge,

One-eighth of a mile below the American cataract, was opened to the public on the 4th day of January, 1869.

It is the longest suspension bridge in the world; its roadway being 1300 feet in length. Its cables are 1800 feet in length; the towers 100 feet high, and it spans the mighty chasm through which rolls its floods towards Lake Ontario, 190 feet above the water.

From this bridge the most delightful views of the Falls are to be obtained, as well as of the great ravine between the Canadian Fall and the Rapids, a distance of two miles, along the bottom of which the vast drainage of the upper inland seas flows in a stream 250 feet in depth. It is but a walk of twenty minutes from the principal hotels on the American side to the former site of Table Rock and the Horse Shoe Fall on the Canada side.

As a work of engineering art and mechanical skill, it adds a new attraction to the scenery which excites the admiration of every beholder, and is indeed the envy of all other nations.

Biddle's Stairs.

These Stairs take their name from the well-known president of the United States Bank, Nicholas Biddle, Esq., at whose expense they were erected in 1829.

They are secured to the solid rock by ponderous iron bolts, and are said to be perfectly safe. The perpendicular height of the bank at this place is 185 feet; the staircase itself being eighty feet high, and consisting of ninety steps. From the stairs to the river there is a rude pathway; but it is seldom traversed, except for the purpose of angling, an art which, at the right time of the year, is here practiced with the happiest success.

In 1829, shortly after the completion of the stairs, the eccentric Sam Patch, of saltatory memory, made his famous leap from a scaffolding ninety-six feet high, erected in the water at a point between this and the Center Fall.

From the foot of Biddle's Stairs two paths lead in opposite directions, one toward the Canada, and the other toward the American Fall. The former has been obstructed by slides from above, and is not, perhaps, altogether safe. Taking the latter, a few minutes' walk brings you to the celebrated Cave of the Winds. If you have provided dresses, you here enter by a secure stairway. The formation of this cave was of easy process. The gradual wearing away by the water of the shaly substratum of the precipice has left the limestone rock above projecting at least 30 feet beyond the base; thus forming an open cave, over which falls in deep folds of

Æolus's Cave — Byron's Description of Cascade of Velino.

azure, the magnificent curtain of the Center Fall. The compression of the atmosphere by the falling water is here so great that the cave is rendered as stormy and turbulent as that of old Æolus himself, from whose classical majesty, indeed, it derived its first name —

Æolus's Cave.

Gazing now below you at that delicate textured rainbow trembling in the angry surge, you will hardly fail to remember Byron's vivid description of the bow at the cascade of Velino:

> " From side to side, beneath the glittering morn,
> An Iris sits, amidst the infernal surge,
> Like hope upon a death bed, and, unworn
> Its stealy dyes, while all around is torn

The Precipice — Goldsmith's Description.

> By the distracted waters, bears serene
> Its brilliant hues with all their beams unshorn;
> Resembling, 'mid the torture of the scene,
> Love watching madness with unalterable mien."

Ascending Biddle's Stairs, your course conducts you to the right, along the verge of the precipice. Observe how the bank is gradually wearing away, by slides of land and crumbling of rocks, from its side. It was near these stairs that the crash occurred in 1843. The detached rock now lies at the foot of the staircase.

By the time you have reached the other side of the island you will be prepared to duly appreciate the estimate of its width, with which Dr. Goldsmith edified the ingenuous youth of his time: "Just in the middle of this circular wall of waters, a little island that has braved the fury of the current presents one of its points, and divides the stream at top into two parts; but they unite again long before they reach the bottom." Its width is, in fact, from fall to fall, seventy-five rods. Some ambitious candidate for applause, in speaking of this island, has called it "the forehead of Niagara, and the cataracts on either side, her streaming hair, puffed up *a la* Jenny Lind, and tied back with rainbows." But you have, by this time, reached the south-western corner of the island. Be seated in the arbor near by, if you please, and we will pay the highest possible compliment to yourself, while gracefully acknowledging our own impressions of the scene, by — silence. There are many descriptions of the Falls; but they are all too lucklessly true to the *form* of their subject — oceans

Description of the Falls — Horseshoe Fall — Prospect Tower.

of sublimity falling into perilous depths of pathos. It may, however, be remarked in passing, that, take whatever point of view we may, we find Nature here expressing herself in bold and beautiful antitheses; the Titanic strength and majesty of the cataract, and the soft, grovy tendrils that bathe their verdure in its spray,— the wild, distracted, maniac surge, and the delicate rainbow shivering in its embrace,— the whirlwind roar of falling floods, and the braided lullaby of lapsing streams. Niagara is all antitheses, all "contrasted charms!" This is commonly called the Horseshoe Fall, a name derived from the shape that the curve formerly assumed. The gradual wearing away from beneath, and falling down from above of the rocks, has now changed the figure from that of a horseshoe to something more nearly resembling that of a right angle.

The width of this fall is about 144 rods; its height, 158 feet. The depth of the water in the center, or deepest part of the stream, is estimated at twenty feet. That light-house looking structure built out in the water, two or three rods from the Fall, is called

Prospect Tower.

It was erected in 1833, by the late Judge Porter. Its height is forty-five feet. The bridge leading from the island to Prospect Tower is called

Terrapin Bridge.

This Bridge is subject to the action of the spray; a

Terrapin Bridge — Accident — Fall of a portion of Rock.

little care should therefore be taken in crossing it. In the winter of 1852, a gentleman from West Troy, N. Y., while crossing to the tower, fell into the current, and was carried to the verge of the fall, where he lodged between two rocks. He was discovered by two of the citizens, who rescued him by throwing out lines which he fastened around his body. He remained speechless for several hours after being taken to his hotel.

From the tower, you get the best view of the shape of the fall, and the clearest idea of how it has been modified by the action of the water. This action has been especially violent during the last few years. On Sunday, Feb. 1, 1852, a portion of the precipice, stretching from the edge of the island toward the tower, about 125 feet long and sixty feet wide, and reaching from near the top to the bottom of the fall, fell with a crash of thunder. The next day another, a triangular piece, with a base of about forty feet, broke off just below the tower. Between the two portions that had thus fallen off, stood a rectangular projection about thirty feet long and fifteen feet wide, extending from the top to the bottom of the precipice. This immense mass became loosened from the main body of the rock, and settled perpendicularly about eight feet, where it now stands, an enormous column 150 feet high by the dimensions named above.

The line of division between the government of the United States and that of Canada is in the deepest part of the channel, or through the angular part of the fall.

The Three Sisters — Narrow Escape — Moss Island.

Leaving Prospect Tower and the Horseshoe Fall, and wending our way along the bank of the river to the east, the next great point of interest is (*See page* 32.)

The Three Sisters.

These are three small islands, lying side by side, near the head of Goat Island. The remotest of this trinity is the island from which Mr Joel R. Robinson rescued a Mr. Allen in the summer of 1841. Mr. Allen, having started just before sundown for Chippewa, (a village three miles up the river on the Canada side,) had the misfortune to break one of his oars in the midst of the river. The current caught his boat and bore it rapidly toward the Falls. As his only hope of safety, he steered with the remaining oar for the head of Goat Island; but failing to strike that, he was bearing swiftly past this little island, when, knowing that the alternative was certain doom, he sprang for the land, and reached it with but little injury. Having matches in his pocket, he struck a signal light at the head of the island, but it was not seen until morning. Mr. Robinson rescued him by means of a boat and cable.

The first of the sisterhood, or the island nearest you, is called Moss Island. That feathery show of a cataract between yourself and Moss Island is called the Hermit's Cascade, from its having been the usual bathing-place of

Francis Abbott, the Hermit of Niagara.

Beside his once favorite haunt, we will, with your permission, relate his story. The history of this

The Hermit of Niagara.

singular individual has been given in various forms, from the hurried compilation of a guide-book to the extravagances of a romance. We present you with what is known of him by all who lived in the village at the time of his residing here.

His first appearance at Niagara was in the afternoon of June 18, 1839. He was a young man then, tall and well-formed, but emaciated and haggard; of an easy and gentlemanly deportment, but sufficiently eccentric in appearance to arrest a stranger's gaze.

Clad in a long, flowing robe of brown, and carrying under his arm a roll of blankets, a book, portfolio, and flute, he proceeded to a small, retired inn, where he engaged a room for a week, stipulating, however, that the room was to be, for the time, exclusively *his*, and that only a *part* of his food was to be prepared by the family. Soon after, he visited the village library, entered his name, and drew books. He also purchased a violin. At the expiration of a week he returned to the library, where, falling into conversation, he spoke with much enthusiasm on the subject of the Falls, and expressed his intention of remaining here some time longer.

Shortly afterward he asked permission of the proprietor of these islands to erect a cabin on Moss Island, that he might live in greater seclusion than the village afforded him. Failing in his request, he took up his abode in part of a small log-house, then standing near the head of Goat Island. Here for nearly two years he continued to live, with no companions

The Hermit of Niagara.

but his dog, his books, and music—blameless but almost unknown. On this island, at hours when it was unfrequented by others, he delighted to roam, heedless, if not oblivious of danger. At that time a stick of timber about eight inches square extended from Terrapin Bridge eight feet beyond the precipice. On this he has been seen at almost all hours of the night, pacing to and fro beneath the moonlight, without the slightest apparent tremor of nerve or hesitancy of step. Sometimes he might be seen sitting carelessly on the extreme end of the timber—sometimes hanging beneath it by his hands and feet. Although exquisitely sensitive in his social habits, he seems to have been without an apprehension in the presence of danger. After residing on Goat Island two winters, he crossed Bath Island Bridge, and built him a rude cabin of boards at Point View, near the American Fall. (*Vide p.* 36.) Although brought into the immediate neighborhood of the villagers, he held but little intercourse with them; sometimes, indeed, refusing to break his silence by oral communication with any one. At times, however, he was extremely affable to all, easily drawn into conversation, and supporting it with a regard to conventionalism, and a grace and accuracy of expression that threw a charm over the most trivial subject of remark.

The late Judge De Vaux was perhaps the only person with whom he was really familiar. With him he would often interchange arguments, by the hour, on some point of theology—his favorite topic of discussion. His views on this subject were by no means stable; but as far as they assumed a definite form they seemed nearly akin to those held by the Society of Friends. But it was in his brilliant reminiscences of foreign lands and scenes that he was especially glorious. All his subjective speculations were tinged by shadows of melancholy or despair; but in describing the glories of nature and art, the scholar and the amateur lifted off the cowl of the hermit, and revealed the enthusiasm of a spirit still exquisitely alive to the kindling touch of Beauty. He had wandered among the ruins of Asia and Greece, and studied the trophies of art in the celebrated picture galleries of Italy.

Of music he was passionately fond, and played his own compositions, in the opinion of some, with exquisite taste; while others declare his execution to have been only mediocre, if not absolutely inferior.

Every day, after his removal to the main-land, it was his custom to descend the ferry stairs to bathe in the river below; and it was while thus engaged that he was accidentally drowned, June 10, 1841. Ten days afterward his body was found at the outlet of the river, and brought back to the village, where it was committed to the earth in sight of the scenes he so much loved.

After his decease a number of citizens repaired to his cabin to take charge of his effects. Little however was to be found: his faithful dog guarded the door; his cat lay on the lounge; and his books and music were scattered around the room. Writing was sought for in vain. It is said, notwithstanding, that he wrote much, but always in Latin, and committed

The Hermit of Niagara

his productions to the flames almost as soon as composed.

You will now ask, "What caused him to lead the life of a hermit?" This question has never been answered. It is commonly supposed that he had been the victim of some disappointment; but we have nothing to relieve the supposition. Members of his family have, since his death, visited Niagara; from whom we learn only that Francis was a son of the late John Abbott, of Plymouth, England, a member of the Society of Friends, and that in his youth he alternated the most indefatigable devotion to his studies with the most excessive dissipations of a gay metropolis. If we were to decide from our present knowledge of his history, we should say that his social eccentricities were owing rather to the constitutional tendencies of his mind, developed by the tenor of his early life, than to any one controlling circumstance; that study, dissipation, and, possibly, disappointments, had so far destroyed the harmony of both mind and body, that, with Childe Harold before him, he

"From his native land resolved to go,
 And visit scorching climes beyond the sea;
 With pleasure drugged, he almost longed for woe,
 And e'en for change of scene, would seek the shades below."

We have given only what we *know* of his life. There still remains a wide margin which each may fill up, as best suits himself, with the speculations of romance.

Gallant Feat of Mr. Robinson.

Begging your pardon for detaining you here so long, let us continue our course around the island.

On this rise of ground, a few rods above the Hermit's Cascade, pause a moment, while we relate a gallant feat performed here in June, 1854. A large sand-scow had broken loose from its moorings, and lodged between two rocks nearly opposite the head of the island, and in range with the furthest of the Three Sisters. Property was on board, and Mr. Robinson consented to undertake to save it. Accordingly, in the presence of hundreds of spectators, accompanied by his son, he pushed his skiff from the head of the island, struck out above the boat, and then dropped down the current. With incredible quickness the son sprang from the skiff at the right moment, and secured it to the scow. *But how to return!* Strangers said that *he couldn't do it.* Those who knew Mr. R. felt that he *would*, while they wondered how he *could!* Below him is a cascade eight feet high; there is danger of his going over that, and then—but meanwhile the father is again in the skiff, and now the son loosens the fastening, and there they go like thought. "*They're lost!*" runs through the crowd on shore. They are nearing the fall; in a second they are on its brink, and—a graceful touch of the oars, and the flying boat is as motionless as if on land. Their skiff is poised on the very verge of that wild cascade; "but they can return," was now the hope and thought of all. Quickly they lift their oars—and quickly are lost in the dashing surge.

View from Head of Goat Island.

They are not *lost* long, however; for, landing on the second "Sister," they carry their boat to the foot of that island, launch it again in the waves, and careering in a bold sweep through the rapids, reach the shore amid deafening plaudits.

A few rods further on, and you have reached the

Head of Goat Island.

This point commands a comprehensive view in outline of the river and its environs for some miles of its course. Looking up the right bank, you behold, at a distance of about a mile, a small, white farm-house, with a chimney of most disproportionate size. This

SCHLOSSER LANDING.

is the site of old Fort Schlosser, a name celebrated in border story. That towering chimney was taken entire from the mess-house attached to the establishment. This fort was built at an early date by the French, and called by them Little Fort. At the end of the Anglo-French war in America, it was ceded to the English, and was first occupied as a military post by Capt. Schlosser, from whom it derived its second name. One mile above Fort Schlosser is *Schlosser Landing*. In a diagonal direction from this point, and near the Canada shore, is

Navy Island.

This island has an area of 304 acres, and belongs to the realms of Her Britannic Majesty. It is closely associated with Schlosser by an affair which, as it has not yet found its way into the pages of Bancroft or Hildreth, we will briefly relate: In 1837, a rebellion was stirred up against the authorities of Canada, by some disaffected "Radicals," under the leadership of Wm. Lyon McKenzie and some others; but, Her Majesty's subjects not caring to side with the "Rebels" in any great number, the movement was speedily put down. But not so the leaders. They — *i. e.* McKenzie, Gen. Sutherland, and five or six and twenty others — at the suggestion of a Dr. Chapin of Buffalo, unfurled the standard of rebellion over this island, designing to make it a *rendezvous* for the restlessly patriotic of both sides of the river, until sufficient strength should be gained to renew the attack. Matters were going on pleasantly — the "Patriots" being daily edified by accessions to their strength, though greatly demoralized by a barrel of whisky that found its way to their panting hearts — when the difficulty of "transporting volunteers and supplies to their place of destination," and "the number of persons from motives of business or curiosity constantly desirous of passing and repassing from the main-land to the patriot camp, suggested to

Machination of Sir Allan McNab.

Mr. Wells, the owner of a small steamboat lying at Buffalo, called the Caroline, the idea of taking out the necessary papers, and running his vessel as a ferry-boat between the American shore and the islands, for his own pecuniary emolument."* Accordingly, Friday, December 29, the Caroline left Buffalo for Schlosser; and after having arrived, having made several trips during the day, on account of the owner, was moored to the wharf at Schlosser Landing during the night.

Colonel Sir Allan McNab, then commanding at Chippewa a detachment of Her Majesty's forces, having got word of the enterprise of the Caroline, resolved upon a deed which relieves the farcical story of the rebellion by a dash of genuine outrage. It is asserted that Sir Allan was informed that the Caroline was in the interest of the Patriots, chartered for their use, and intended to act offensively against the Canadian authorities. Whether this be true or not, he planned her destruction that very night. For this purpose, a chosen band is detailed, and placed under the command of a Captain Drew, a retired-on-half-pay officer of the royal navy.

At midnight the captain received his parting orders from Sir Allan, and the chivalrous band departed in eight boats for the scene of their gallant daring.

The unconscious Caroline, meanwhile, lay peacefully at her moorings, beneath the stars and stripes of her country's banner. As the tavern at Schlosser — the

---

* Peck's Tourist's Companion.

Seizure of the Caroline — The Burning Boat.

only building near by — could accommodate but a limited number of persons, several had sought a night's lodging within the sides of the boat. Dreaming of no danger, they had retired to rest unprovided with arms. Thus was the night wearing on, when so stealthily came the hostile band that the faint plash of muffled oars was the first intimation the sentry had of their approach. In reply to his question, "Who goes there?" came, first, "*Friends!*" then, a heavy plashing in the water; then, the leaping of armed men to the deck. The bewildered sleepers start from their dreams and rush for the shore. "Cut them down!" shrieks the heroic Drew, as he thrills with the memory of Aboukir and the Nile —"Cut them down, give no quarter." More or less injured, they escape to the shore, with life — all but one, Durfee, the last man to leave, who is brought to the earth by a pistol-shot, a corpse!

A few minutes and the Caroline moves from the shore in flames! Down the wild current she speeds faster and faster, flinging flames in her track, till striking the Canada waters she spurns the contact, leaps like a mad fury, and in a moment more is as dark as the night around her. The common account of this affair takes it for granted that the boat went over the Canada Fall aflame. You will read of the fated vessel lifting her fairy form to the verge of the precipice, lighting up the dark amphitheater of cataracts, etc., to the end of endurance. The case was far otherwise. The physician who was called to the wounded at Schlosser was riding up the river's bank while the Caroline was

City of Ararat — Burning of Store-ships.

descending the rapids. This gentleman testifies that the boat, a perfect mass of illumination, her timbers all aflame, and her pipes red hot, instantly expired when she struck the cascade below the head of Goat Island.

Grand Island

Lies not far above Navy Island, is twelve miles in length, and from two to seven in breadth. The land is highly fertile, and much of it is in actual state of cultivation. It was on this island that the late Major Mordecai M. Noah, of New York, designed to build the "City of Ararat," as a place of refuge for the scattered tribes of Israel. In 1825, he even went so far as to lay the corner-stone, amid infinite pomp, and to erect a monument commemorative of the occasion. The monument is still standing, in excellent state of preservation.

At the foot of this island lies BUCKHORN ISLAND, with an area of about 300 acres. Between these two islands is an arm of the river, deep and clear, called

Burnt Ship Bay,

From a circumstance connected with the close of the French war in 1759. The garrison at Schlosser had already made a gallant resistance to one attack of the English, and were preparing for another, when, disheartened by the news of the fall of Quebec, they resolved to destroy the two armed vessels containing their military stores. Accordingly, they brought them to this bay and set them on fire. The wrecks, even at this day, are sometimes visible.

The Three Sister Bridges.

The greatest attraction that come in with the pleasure season of 1868, was the "Sister Bridges."

These costly and substantial structures, built over the three channels which separate the Three Sisters from each other, and from Goat Island, presenting new and grand views of the Rapids and Falls, unequalled from any other point. These three bridges combine both strength and beauty They are alike, being slightly oval, that is, higher in the middle than at either end, thus adding to their strength. The ends are fastened into the solid rock. Two rods, two inches in diameter, pass under each bridge, and are also fastened in the rocks at either end. The peculiar construction of the railing adds much to strength and beauty. Pass over each bridge slowly, and carefully view the Rapids and Cascades — views never before made apparent to the eye. Here Joel R. Robinson, in 1841, saved a Mr. Allen's life (see page 21), and in 1854 he passed with his son over the Rapids (see page 26). A fourth island, or sister, was discovered while the bridges were being built; to it a bridge has also been thrown. All lovers should pass over to the gem, and christen it as "The Lovers' Resort." From the head of the third sister may be seen one continuous cascade or fall, extending as far as the eye can reach, from Goat Island across to the Canada shore, varying from ten to twenty feet in height. From this miniature Niagara rises a spray similar to that of the great Falls. The Rapids here are very fine, surpassing in volume the rapids under Goat Island Bridge, and much more beautiful in appearance.

The pleasure of passing over these wild and romantic spots fully repays the visitor for the trip, say nothing of the many other beautiful resorts that abound at Niagara, both winter and summer.

A Man in Jeopardy.

On your return from Goat Island to the main-land, nothing requires special notice until you are again crossing Bath Island Bridge. Standing midway between the toll-house and main-land, and looking toward the precipice, you see, at a distance nearly half-way between the bridge and the cataract, a log protruding from amidst the waves. That is the spot so intimately associated with

The Fate of Avery.

On Friday evening, July 19, 1853, two young Germans, belonging to a sand-scow which lay moored for the night at the French Landing, took a small boat attached to the scow, and started out on the river for a pleasure sail. Nothing more is known of them until the next morning, when one of them, Joseph Avery, was discovered clinging to that log; the other had, doubtless been carried over the precipice the evening before. The inmates of the toll-house heard cries through the night, but not suspecting their source, gave them no further heed.

As soon as the peril of the man became known, vast numbers of citizens and strangers thronged to the river's side, anxious to witness his escape. A boat was procured, and let down the current by ropes, but it swamped before reaching him. Another was brought and sent to the log, but the lines attached to it became hopelessly entangled among the rocks. In this way, all the plans of the forenoon miscarried. Early in the afternoon, a stoutly built raft was prepared, and let down

Futile Efforts for his Rescue.

the river till it lay along side the log; to which Avery bound himself with cords provided for that purpose; not touching, however, the food that was also sent him, so anxious was he to escape.

The raft was then drawn slowly toward the shore, but had gone only a little way, when it became immovably fixed in the rocks. The excited throngs that had waited since morning for the rescue of the unhappy man, now doubly moved as hope grew fainter and fainter, prayed passionately for his deliverance. The poor fellow himself labored with all his might, in concert with his helpers on the shore, but in vain. It was nearly sunset when the attempt was finally repeated. A ferry-boat was then brought from the ferry, and sent down toward the raft. Seeing it approach, Avery cut away the cords that bound him, and when it was within a few feet of him, sprang to reach it; but, weakened by long fasting and fatigue, his strength failed him, and he struck the water. Just at this crisis, a young man, breathless with haste, presented himself at the bridge, and applied for admission to the guards who were keeping off the crowd. On being refused, he cried out piteously, in broken accents, "*It is my brother!*" He had heard of his brother's peril in a neighboring city, and had hurried to the scene of danger, only in time to hear that brother hailed by the despairing cries of thousands, and to see him struggling amid the wild waves that soon closed over him forever.

Having now visited the most interesting portion of the scenery on the American side, you will, perhaps,

Ferry Railway and Stairs — Point View.

wish to cross the river, and explore the Canadian bank; if so, for topographical directions, turn to page 45. For convenience of reference, we shall first complete our view of the American side, and then take up the Canadian topics by themselves.

Following the course of the river from the bridge toward the precipice, whether on the bank or through Ferry Grove, a short walk brings you to

The Ferry Railway and Stairs.

Which descend through a cut in the bank to the water's edge, a distance of 360 feet. The spiral stairs constructed here in 1825, having become shaky with age, the present novel but commodious contrivance was inaugurated in 1845. The flight of stairs leading along the railway consists of 290 steps. The car is drawn up the inclined plane by water-power — an overshot-wheel being turned by a stream diverted from the river for that purpose. Around a wheel eight feet in diameter, which turns in a horizontal position at the head of the railway, runs a cable two and a half inches in diameter and 300 feet in length, attached to a car at either end, and supported by pulleys placed at convenient intervals down the grade.

Point View

Is a sudden elevation of the bank a few rods below the ferry-house. A number of years ago, the adjacent grounds were tastefully arranged into a pleasure-garden and bowling-green. Upon this spot stood a

POINT VIEW.

Chinese Pagoda, surmounted by a camera-obscura. A few rods to the east of this stood the cabin of Francis Abbott. *Apropos* of the place, we subjoin

Stanzas

Addressed to the sojourners at Niagara Falls, on commencing building the Pagoda, Aug. 11, 1843.

> Those who have rambled o'er the wild domain,
> And still desire to view it once again,
> Enter the garden where an Abbott dwelt,
> And roam where he, enraptured, gazed and knelt.
> Still, even yet those plaintive strains I hear,
> Which once he wakened — and the pensive tear
> Steals softly o'er my cheek, while the full heart
> Essays to know what sorrow winged the dart
> Which sent him forth, a wanderer from his home,
> 'Mid these majestic scenes in silent grief to roam.

Stanzas addressed to Sojourners — Catlin's Cave.

Say, wanderers! would ye dare the wild excess
Of joy and wonder words can ne'er express?
Would ye fain steal a glance o'er life's dark sea,
And gaze, though trembling, on eternity?
Would ye look out, look down, where God has set
His mighty signet? Come — come higher yet,
And from the unfinished structure gaze abroad,
And wonder at the power of God;
To the Pagoda's utmost height ascend,
And see earth, air, and sky, in one alembic blend!

Up — though the trembling limb and nerveless hand
Strive to detain thee on the solid land;
Up — though the heart may fail, the eye grow dim,
Soon will the spirit nerve the quivering limb.
Up the rude ladder! gain the utmost verge;
Far, far below, behold the angry surge;
Beneath your feet the rainbow's arch declines,
Gleaming with richer gems than India's mines;
And deep within the gulf, yet farther down,
'Mid mist, and foam, and spray, behold Niagara's crown.
ALMIRA.

Catlin's Cave.

Two caves were discovered about three-fourths of a mile below the ferry, in 1825, by a Mr. Catlin of Lockport. The one which bears his name — the larger and more curious of the two — is "a round hollow in the center of a large, and nearly spherical rock, formed by a deposit of calcareous tufa, from the drippings of lime-water springs, which gush out of the rocks in many places at and near the cave." The entrance to this cave is extremely contracted, being hardly large enough to admit a medium sized man; and the cave itself is but little more than ten feet in its greatest dimension. The other, called

Giant's Cave

Is a little distance above the former, and differs from it in being the result of mechanical, as that was of chemical agency. The hollow was formed by the disintegration of a portion of the cliff, and somewhat resembles an immense fireplace. In both of these caves, specimens of petrified moss, and stalactite forms of carbonate of lime are found; but not always.

From the difficulty, if not danger, of reaching these caves, they are seldom visited by strangers, and to most persons would, perhaps, not repay the trouble of a visit.

The Suspension Bridge

Spans the river two miles below the Falls. This stupendous enterprise was commenced in the summer of 1852. It is the work of John A. Roebling, of Trenton, New Jersey, whose distinguished reputation as an engineer has long been established by the successful construction of several of the best known suspension bridges and aqueducts in the United States.

It forms a single span of 800 feet in length between the towers, and consists of two floors; the upper, or railway floor, being eighteen feet above the lower or carriage way. These floors are connected together at the sides by open truss work, so as to form, as it were, an immense car, 800 feet long, 24 feet wide, and 18 feet high — all suspended by wire ropes from four

NIAGARA FROM POINT VIEW.

cables of about ten inches in diameter, each. Two of the cables have a deflection of fifty-four feet, and sustain the upper floor; the remaining two, a deflection of sixty-four feet, and support the lower floor. The connection, however, of the floors by means of the side trusses, is such as to cause an equal strain on both sets of cables, from any load passing over either the upper or lower floor. The cables are composed of No. 9 wire, and are fastened, on both sides of the river, by massive iron chains let down from twenty to thirty feet into the native rock, and resting upon cast-iron saddles on the tops of the towers.

The following statement will be interesting to the general reader, and may be relied on as correct:

The towers are 15 feet square at the base, and 8 feet square at the top.

Height of the American towers above the rock, ... 88 feet.
Height of the Canadian towers above the rock, ... 78 "
Length of each of the upper cables, . 1,256 "
Length of each of the lower cables, . 1,190 "
Average number of wires in each cable, 3,684
Total number of wires in all four cables, 14,736
Number of feet of wire, ... 18,129,004
Number of feet of wire in wire rope, . 3,043,022
Aggregate length of wire, 20,463,422 feet, or more than 4000 miles.
Ultimate capacity of the four cables, 12,400 tons.
Total weight of the Suspension Bridge, 800 "

Suspension Bridge — The Whirlpool.

This ample capacity of the cables will be better appreciated when it is stated that the total weight of a loaded train of double freight cars covering the entire length of the bridge, including the weight of the locomotive, and added to the above weight of the superstructure, would be less than 1300 tons.

The successful completion of this bridge must be considered as a new and most important era in the history of scientific achievement. It presents the suspension principle in a manner decidedly original, and combines, in a most astonishing degree, strength, stiffness, durability, and beauty.

The Whirlpool.

Three miles below the Falls, the river turns abruptly in its course, and springs away to the right. At this point the current breaks against a spur of the Canadian cliff, and a part of it, being thrown to the left, sweeps around in a circular direction before reuniting with the main stream. This circular current is called the Whirlpool.

The Devil's Hole,

Three and a half miles below the Falls, is a large, triangular chasm in the river's bank. Into this chasm falls a small st.eam called the Bloody Run. This place is much resorted to by those curious to see the places where have occured the bloody and

Devil's Hole.

vindictive struggles made by the Indians to resist the steady encroachments of the whites upon their hunting grounds. It was at this place that one of the last efforts was made by the Senecas, the most powerful of the Six Nations, and certainly the accounts of the battle and massacre, as handed down by the traditions of the early settlers, and of the Indians themselves, show that no conflict ever waged by the Indians, exceeded this in the relentless fury and vindictiveness which they exercised in driving the unfortunate whites to the alternative of death by jumping over the fearful precipice, or by the scalping knife.

A gentleman of high respectability, who became a resident in this vicinity in 1799, was present, not long after his arrival, at a friendly interview between Brandt, the Indian chief, and Mr. Steadman, who made his escape from the massacre of the Devil's Hole. From their conversation, he learned the following facts relating to that event: Steadman was in the commissary's department, and had charge of the provision train, then on its route from Fort Niagara to Fort Schlosser, guarded by a company of regular troops and by friendly Indians. When the attack commenced, the train was in, and clustered on each bank of Bloody Run; Steadman being mounted on a powerful black horse, broke through the line, which had completely enclosed the devoted party, and made his escape by the Fort Schlosser

Bloody Run.

road to the south, closely pursued by Brandt and two Indians. After gaining, at his best speed, the high ground near the site of the stone house now occupied by Mr. Vogt, he looked around to ascertain his chances of escape, and discovered that Brandt was in advance, rapidly gaining on him, and that the two Indians had not yet reached the brow of the hill, and were therefore not in sight. In this desperate emergency, he made the masonic signal of distress; whereupon Brandt made a signal of recognition, returned, informed his companions that pursuit was useless, and directed their instant return to the contest still in progress. Steadman had therefore, no further difficulty in effecting his escape to Fort Schlosser.

The party when attacked, being in, and huddled in disorder on the banks of Bloody Run, made no resistance. The first fire of the Indian fusees produced a great destruction of life; the drivers were tomahawked on their seats, and those who were not thus killed, were driven alive over the precipice, together with their teams and baggage. Bloody Run, on this occasion, literally contributed blood instead of water to the dark abyss below, and received at that time its present name.

The drummer belonging to the escort, in falling over the precipice, fell upon his drum in such a way as to prevent any serious injury; and after the enemy had retired, he made his escape out of the Devil's Hole to Fort Niagara. Mr. Steadman and the drummer, whose name was Mathews, were the only survivors of the ambuscaded party.

CANADA SIDE.

Crossing the River.

THE advisable course, we think, is to cross the river at the Ferry in going, and at the Suspension Bridge in returning. The best time for crossing at the Ferry, in summer, is either in the morning, or two or three hours before sunset. If the light is favorable,— and in summer, at these hours, it almost always is,— this crossing will probably afford you your most vivid and lasting impression of the Falls. Nowhere do you have so fine a view of the Falls as *from below*. You may here test in your own experience the worth of Burke's æsthetic principle with regard to height and depth: "I am apt to imagine [Burke on the Sublime and Beautiful, §8,] that height is less grand than depth, and that we are more struck at looking down from a precipice, than looking up at an object of equal height; but of that I am not very sure." This was a necessary result of connecting the feeling of the sublime with that of self-preservation. We doubtless feel more of *terror* (are more "struck") in looking down a depth than up a height; but terror, so far from being a principle, or even a condition of sublimity, can not for a moment coexist with its nobler forms.

Carriages await you at the landing on the Canada side. The distance up the bank from the water's edge to the Clifton House is 160 rods. Proceeding from the Clifton House along the bank toward the Canadian Fall, the first object to arrest your steps is

Barnett's Museum.

This collection of natural and artificial curiosities is well worth seeing. The galleries are arranged to represent a forest scene, filled with beasts, birds, and creeping things. There are, besides, several chained-up ferocities in the yard, and a tastefully arranged green-house in the garden. The admission fee is twenty-five cents.

A few rods below the museum, Miss Martha K. Rugg fell from the bank while attempting to pick a flower that grew on its edge. She was living when reached; but expired soon afterward. This accident occurred Aug. 24, 1844.

Table Rock

Is about twenty rods above the museum, at the angle formed by the Horseshoe Fall with the Canadian bank. The bank here sends out, far beyond the line of its general perpendicular, a regular table-like ledge of rock, in the same plane with the crest of the cataract.

The form and dimensions of Table Rock have been changed by frequent and violent disruptions. In July, 1818, a mass broke off 160 feet in length, and from thirty to forty feet in width. December 9, 1828, three immense portions, reaching under the Horseshoe Fall, fell "with a shock like an earthquake." In the summer

Table Rock — Mrs. Sigourney's Apostrophe to Niagara.

of 1829, another large mass fell off, and June 26, 1850, a piece 200 feet long, 60 feet wide, and 100 feet thick. In the part of Table Rock that still remains there is a fissure 125 feet long, and 60 feet deep. Those who wish to go under the Horseshoe Fall can descend a road, cut from the museum to the foot of the fall. Dresses can be procured and guides obtained to pass under Table Rock.

It was on Table Rock that Mrs. Sigourney wrote her spirited

Apostrophe to Niagara.

Flow on, forever, in thy glorious robe
Of terror and of beauty. God has set
His rainbow on thy forehead, and the clouds
Mantled around thy feet. And He doth give
Thy voice of thunder power to speak of Him
Eternally: — bidding the lip of man
Keep silence, and upon thy rocky altar, pour
Incense of awe-struck praise.
      And who can dare
To lift the insect trump of earthly hope,
Or love, or sorrow, 'mid the peal sublime
Of thy tremendous hymn! Even ocean shrinks
Back from thy brotherhood, and his wild waves
Retire abashed; for he doth sometimes seem
To sleep like a spent laborer, and recall
His wearied billows from their vieing play,
And lull them to a cradle calm: but thou,
With everlasting, undecaying tide,
Dost rest not night nor day.
      The morning stars
When first they sang o'er young creation's birth,
Heard thy deep anthem; and those wrecking fires
That wait the archangel's signal, to dissolve

The solid earth, shall find Jehovah's name
Graven, as with a thousand diamond spears,
On thine unfathomed page. Each leafy bough
That lifts itself within thy proud domain,
Doth gather greenness from thy living spray,
And tremble at the baptism. Lo! yon birds
Do venture boldly near, bathing their wings
Amid thy foam and mist. 'T is meet for them
To touch thy garments here, or lightly stir
The snowy leaflets of this vapor wreath,
Who sport unharmed on the fleecy cloud,
And listen at the echoing gate of heaven
Without reproof. But as for us, it seems
Scarce lawful with our broken tones to speak
Familiarly of thee. Methinks, to tint
Thy glorious features with our pencil's point,
Or woo thee with the tablet of a song,
Were profanation.
    Thou dost make the soul
A wondering witness of thy majesty;
And while it rushes with delirious joy
To tread thy vestibule, dost chain its step,
And check its rapture, with the humbling view
Of its own nothingness, bidding it stand
In the dread presence of the Invisible,
As if to answer to its God through thee.

Burning Spring

Is about one mile above Table Rock, near the river's edge. The water of the spring is highly charged with sulphureted hydrogen gas, and emits a pale, blue light when ignited. To heighten the effect, the phenomenon of the burning water is exhibited in a darkened room.

 Near this spot was fought the battle of Chippewa. July 5, 1814.

BURNING SPRING.

Lunday's Lane Battle Ground—Bender's Cave—Village Niagara Falls.

Lunday's Lane Battle Ground

Is one mile and a half westwardly from the Falls. On this plain was fought the great battle of the war of 1814, July 25. The loss on both sides, in killed and wounded, was nearly 1800. The village near by is Drummondville, in memory of Gen. Drummond, the commandor of the British forces on the line.

Bender's Cave

Is one mile below the Clifton House, and twenty feet below the top of the bank. The cave is a natural hollow in the rock, in shape somewhat resembling a large oven, and measuring forty feet in breadth and depth. Hermits are respectfully invited to call and examine.

We soon come to the great International Suspension Bri'ge, (see description elsewhere,) two miles below Niagara Falls. Cross over and proceed to the

Village of Niagara Falls.

This place is not yet large, it is true, but its recent growth has been extremely rapid. Within the last ten years its population has increased from one thousand to nearly three thousand persons. Buildings have everywhere sprung up, and yet not enough to meet the demand. The peculiarities of the place adapt it to all classes of persons — to the adventurer, the

Village of Niagara Falls — Niagara by Moonlight.

capitalist, the amateur, the rigid utilitarian, and the lover of elegant retirement. One great cause of its present prosperity is found in the energetic efforts now making to render available for mechanical purposes the vast wealth of natural power that has here slumbered for ages. An instance of this is the hydraulic canal now in process of cutting, from a point about a mile above the precipice to a point a half a mile below it. The completion of this enterprise is confidently awaited as the beginning of a new era in the industrial history of this part of the country. The village is not yet large enough to render a particular account of its topography necessary. The stores and hotels are situated principally on Main Street. The churches stand on the street immediately in the rear; that is, to the east of this. The new stone church belongs to the Methodist denomination; the large stone one, with the town clock in its steeple, to the Presbyterian; the brown church, surmounted by a cross, to the Episcopalian; and the white stone building north of this, to the Baptist. The Romish church stands back of the third street in the rear of this.

Niagara by Moonlight.

There is much the same difference between Niagara in the "gairish light of day" and Niagara bathed in the soft splendor of moonlight, that there would be between the Paradise Lost in the freedom of its epic grandeur and the same translated into vapid prose. The peculiar charm of the scene is not in the separate enjoyment of the silvery light and of the forceful flood, nor yet in any contrast between the grace of the one and the strength of the other, but in the instantaneous blending of complementary influences, a sort of "gladness in accomplished promise." The peculiar effect of moonlight upon the features of a landscape is to harmonize, to soften, to spiritualize. Every thing within its smile is lighter and more graceful. The rivers are turned into "vales of winding light;" the cliffs loose their harshness of outline; the trees, in their picturesque repose, look like the trees of a dream; even sound itself, in sympathy with the scene, falls upon the ear with softer cadence. A favorite haunt at Niagara in this magical season is Goat Island. It is here that the best views are obtained of that rare phenomenon, the Lunar Bow. At the time of the full moon this exhibition is as perfect as lunar light can make it. At best, however, it is very faint, a mere belt of the saintly hue. Many persons consider the lunar bow a sufficient justification of immoderate raptures; but its attractiveness, we can not but think, is owing more to its being so seldom seen than to any intrinsic beauty it may possess.

Indian Tradition.

In connection with a list of the casualties at the Falls, it is usual to mention a tradition among the Indians that at least two persons must annually be sacrificed to the Great Spirit of these waters. The limit on one side, at least, has often been too sadly transcended.

Niagara in Winter.

Comparatively few persons know any thing of the indescribable grandeur of Niagara in winter. The most appreciative of those who have seen it at this season pronounce the view superior, in its kind, to that of the summer scene. We copy the following from the editorial colums of the *Louisville Journal*. It is worthy the pen of its poet editor.

"No one truly appreciates Niagara who has not seen it in midwinter. Deeply as the manifold grandeur and beauty of its summer aspect impresses the beholder, and solemn and delicious as are the emotions it inspires when arrayed in the rich drapery of autumn, it is still more impressive when clad in the superb and dazzling livery of winter. There are few who have had the fortune or the hardihood to visit the great cataract at all seasons, who will not heartily unite in this judgment. We have looked upon it every month in the year, and under almost every possible relation, and never without a sense of strange, inexpressible elevation, such as one might experience in the actual presence of the Infinite; but at no period have we ever felt so exalted and transported by its magical sublimity as in the depth of winter. There is at this time a universal bleakness which repels the vision from discursive movement, and concentrates it, with overwhelming effect, upon the brilliant spectacle of the cataract itself; and certainly that spectacle is among the most striking and splendid of earthly scenes. We know of no mere physical appearance that can rival it in those features which impress the human mind most deeply and permanently.

"Its wonderful enchantment is chiefly due to the gradual freezing of the spray, blown thinly over the islands and adjacent shores, until the simplest objects assume the most grotesque or significant forms, shaped in transparent ice. Very marvelous is the change to one who stood by that majestic tide in the bright hours of August or October. The islands that were then carpeted with verdure, and beaming with the soft tints of summer, are now laid in ice as pure and solid as the most stainless Parian; while the trees and shrubs, that so lately blazed with the splendors of autumn, are robed in the same spotless vesture, and borne down to the very ground by its massy weight. Even the giant rocks that shoot up so boldly from the far depths of the precipice are hooded and wrapped with vast breadths of ice, as if to rebuke their fantastic impertinence. All things are incased and enveloped with gleaming ice. Ice islands are covered with forests of ice that bend down to the ice with the iciest of fruits. Everywhere but in the immediate channel of the swollen and surging river, the ice-giant reigns sovereign of the ascendant — as sovereign as the Scandinavian mythology would have him reign in the generation of the universe. Indeed, when one looks over this shivering but radiant scene, it is easy to sympathize with the ancient Scalds, who held ice to be the primeval matter.

"One of the most singular effects of this frosty

Niagara in its Winter Robes.

dominion is displayed upon Luna Island, (of beautiful memory,) where the trees are bowed down to the earth with their snowy vestments, like so many white nuns doing saintly homage to the genius of the place. But the most magnificent and bewitching effect is produced by the morning sun when it pours over these fairy-like islands and forests a flood of kindling rays. At such a moment the characteristic attributes of Niagara seem fused and heightened into 'something more exquisite still.' Its intrinsic sublimity and beauty experience a literal transfiguration. Nature is visibly idealized. Nothing more brilliant or enchanting can be conceived. The brightest tales of magic 'pale their ineffectual fires.' Islands, whose flowers are thickset with diamonds, and forests, whose branches are glittering with brilliants, and amethysts, and pearls, seem no longer a luxurious figment of genius, but a living and beaming reality. One feels in the midst of such blazing coruscations and such glorious bursts of radiance as if the magician's ring had been slipped upon his finger unawares, and, rubbed unwittingly, had summoned the gorgeous scene before him. It is as if Mammoth Cave, with its groves of stalactites, and crystal bowers, and gothic avenue and halls, and star chambers, and flashing grottoes, were suddenly uncapped to the wintry sun, and bathed in his thrilling beams; or as if the fabled palace of Neptune had risen abruptly from the deep, and were flinging its splendors in the eye of heaven.

"It is indeed a scene of peerless grandeur, and would richly repay a pilgrimage from the extremest limits of the nation. A man of taste and feeling should be willing to 'put a girdle round the globe' to witness it. We are amazed that parties of enterprising tourists do not flock there from all quarters of the Union. They surely have little passion for tne sublime and beautiful who think of the scene only to shudder at it and forgoe it.

"A recent visitor to Niagara states that ne found himself preceded a few days by a large party from the sunny region of Barbadoes. We suppose that, since the hurricane season is over, the gay adventurers of that beautiful island are dying of *ennui*. They can hardly find a nobler substitute for their loved whirlwinds and tornadoes than Niagara in its winter robes.

Hackmen and Guides.

Complaints are frequently made by strangers of being outrageously *gulled* by hackmen and guides. This complaint is a general one, and there is no reason for making it with peculiar emphasis at Niagara. The experienced tourist will always settle the price beforehand, and so avoid any unpleasant scene at the end of his trip. This precaution, so regularly observed in all other matters, should not be omitted in this; the *price* of a thing should be known before we engage to *pay* for it. The usual charge for carriages is two dollars an hour. The compensation for the service of guides is less definitely fixed. Other complaints of a less specific character, are also often made: such as, "a quarter is demanded at every corner," &c. The truth is, no more

Charges of Servants, etc.—Retrocession of the Falls.

money is asked here than elsewhere for an equal, or perhaps less amount of value received; but the greater part of the world are so much accustomed to consider a tangible material return as the only form of the *quid pro quo*, that they cannot understand how so gross an affair as money should enter into considerations of this kind, and consequently regret its expenditures the more keenly.

Retrocession of the Falls.

We copy the following from Profs. Gray & Adams' Geology: "One of the most magnificent and instructive examples of the denuding agency of rivers is to be seen in the retrocession of the *Niagara Falls*, which have cut an enormous ravine from Queenstown, seven miles back to their present situation. Soft shales at the base of the falls underlie the harder limestone, which is gradually undermined, and fragments of the overlying rock are detached from above. In this way, the falls are now retrograding at a rate not easily reckoned with precision for the want of historical data, but variously estimated to average from one foot to one yard per year As the rocks have a small dip backward in the direction of Lake Erie, the water will at length cease to act on the soft shales for the want of sufficient fall below to remove the materials. The process will therefore be arrested long before the falls can have traveled as far as the lake."

Quantity of Water.

In crossing the river just below the falls, the view is justly regarded as one of the most sublime in the natural world. As you look up from the deep ravine, you see at least 20,000,000 cubic feet of water each minute rushing down from a height of 160 feet, and appearing in truth

> "As if God poured it from his 'hollow hand'
> —and had bid
> Its flood to chronicle the ages back,
> And notch his centuries in the eternal rock."

TABLE ROCK.

NIAGARA INTERNATIONAL SUSPENSION BRIDGE.

The Niagara Frontier.

After the battle of Chippewa, Gen. Brown wrote to a friend, from his encampment at Queenston, as follows: "I have now seen the Falls of Niagara in all their majesty, and my camp is situated in a region affording the most sublime and beautiful scenery. I can fancy nothing equal to it, except the noble contest of gallant men on the field of battle, struggling for their country's glory, and their own." The region to which this tribute so gracefully alludes, the Niagara frontier, it is the design of this section to briefly sketch in its local character and historical relations. Niagara river, from lake to lake, comprehends a length of only about thirty-six miles. Contracted as this border region is, as an important section of the geographical line between governments that have not always been on terms of amity, it has often been made the theater of war. Its localities are therefore associated with the history of our country, and with the fame of her military chieftains, and on this, if on no other account, are worthy a description. The history of this region discloses to our view, first, the lordly Indian roaming the majestic solitude; next, the wary pioneers of the civilization and the vices of Europe, mingling the hereditary hatred of their respective nations when crossing one another's path; then a protracted strife for the mastery between the delegated powers of those nations; then a lull of peace and prosperity; again the atrocities of war; and again and now the blessings of peace.

History of the Five Nations—The Iroquois.

First, our immediate predecessors,

The Iroquois.

This was the name given by the French to the confederacy of the Five Nations, consisting of the Mohawks, on the river of that name, the Oneidas, on the southern shore of Oneida lake, the Cayugas, near Cayuga lake, and the Senecas, stretching from the Seneca lake to the Niagara river. Father Hennepin says that there were villages of the Senecas on the Niagara, not many miles above the falls. The Iroquois Senecas were therefore the immediate predecessors of the whites on this frontier. Remnants of this once mighty people, whom Volney, in a burst of enthusiasm, called the ROMANS OF THE WEST, still linger around their primeval homesteads. The Tuscaroras, a tribe incorporated with the Iroquois in 1712, still enjoy the *reservation* of their lands, and occupy a village about nine miles from the Falls. The remains of the Senecas dwell further to the south. It is a curious fact that while the rapacity of the white man has stripped them almost entirely of their possessions, and shorn them of their power, their ancient league is still in force, their traditional customs still observed. Yearly they glide to their council-fire, through the waving grain-lands of their once forest home, like lingering spirits of the past, to banquet on the recollections of their traditionary greatness. "From their ancient seat at Onondaga, the council-fire is transferred to Tonawanda. Here their representatives yet assemble and perform their ancient rites and ceremonies."

It must not, however, be inferred that the Iroquois Senecas were the original proprietors of the soil, or the first of whom we have any account. Just above the horizon of history flits the shadow of a great and peaceful tribe,

The Neuter Nation,

Supposed to be identical with the Kah-Kwas, "in whose wigwams the fierce Hurons and relentless Iroquois met on *neutral ground.*" Father L'Allemant, in 1641, mentions distinctly "the easternmost village of the Neutral Nation, 'Ongniaarha,' (Niagara,) of the same name as the river." In the following year Charlevoix also mentions this people, and says that they were called "'neutral' because they took no part in the wars which desolated the country." Canada West was the seat of the "fierce Hurons." Situated between this warlike people and the Iroquois, the neutrality of the Kah-Kwas could not long be preserved. "To avoid the fury of the Iroquois they joined them against the Hurons, but gained nothing by the union." They fell victims to the furious power they sought to conciliate, and disappeared as a nation about the year 1643. To their seats, as we have said, succeeded the Senecas, who were in occupation of them, when first visited by

The European Pioneers.

It is not known when this region was first visited by

First Settlements — Expedition of La Salle.

Europeans, though such an event was *possible* any time after the discovery of the St. Lawrence, in 1534.

"French traders are said to have visited the Falls as early as 1610 and '15, but there are no authentic accounts to confirm this statement." Side by side with the French trader came the missionary priest,—first the humble Franciscan, and then the wary disciple of Loyola. Father L'Allemant, writing of the Neuter Nation from St. Mary's Mission in 1641, says: "Although many of our French in that quarter have visited this people to profit by their furs and other commodities, we have no knowledge of any who have been there to preach the gospel except Father De La Roch Daillon, a recollet, who passed the winter there in the year 1626." This good father was probably the first European in western New York, and even of him it is said "there is no evidence that he ever saw the Falls." In the fall of 1640, two missionary fathers, Jean de Breboeuf and Joseph Marie Chaumont found their way to some part of this region, but if they saw the Falls they made no mention of them. In 1660, Ducreux wrote a work called "Historiæ Canadensis," and noted the Falls on a map; but the probability is that he took them from hearsay, as he makes no allusion to them in his narrative.

The Expedition of La Salle.

Robert Cavalier de La Salle, a native of France, set out for the new world in 1667. Following up the St. Lawrence, he explored Lake Ontario, and ascended to Lake Erie. La Salle had heard from the Indians of the majestic Ohio, and of the fertile regions beyond; and in the mind of this man was first formed the project of uniting Canada with the valley of the Mississippi by a chain of military posts. Presenting his plans in a memorial to his government, and obtaining a commission for the exploration of the Father of Waters, he set out on his expedition in the fall of 1678, with a numerous band of followers, among whom was Tonti, the Italian, and Father Hennepin. Touching at the present site of Fort Niagara, he there established a trading post. Making the portage from Lewiston to Cayuga creek, on the American side, the whole company improved the opportunity of viewing the Falls. Good Father Hennepin was quite bowed down beneath their grandeur. He is confident that they are above six hundred feet high, and describes them as "a vast and prodigious cadence of water, which falls down after a surprising and astonishing manner, insomuch that the universe does not afford its parallel." As they purposed visiting the head waters of the Mississippi, it was necessary first to build a suitable vessel to navigate the upper lakes. Accordingly a vessel of sixty tons burden was built at the mouth of the Cayuga creek, on the American side of the river, about five miles above the Falls. The vessel was named the "Griffin," in allusion to the arms of the Count de Frontenac, the early patron of La Salle. On the 7th of August, 1679, amid the firing of guns, and the singing of the *Te Deum*, the Griffin lifted her sails to the breeze— the first keel to enter the waters of the upper lakes.

Expedition of De Nouville against the Indians.

The Expedition of De Nonville.

When Champlain came out from France in 1603, he unwisely made the Iroquois the deadly enemies of the French, by actively co-operating with the Hurons against them. This course of policy had been afterward pursued as a tradition, and when the Marquis de Nonville succeeded to the government of New France, in 1685, he found himself involved in a war with the Iroquois, in defense of his Indian allies of the west. He at once resolved to attack the Senecas first, and to build a fort at Niagara, where La Salle had left a trading post. "The commandants of the French posts at the west were ordered to rendezvous at Niagara, with their troops, and the warriors of their Indian allies in that quarter." The French army set out from Montreal on the 13th of June, and reached Irondequoit, on the southern shore of Lake Ontario, on the 12th of July. According to previous arrangement, the commandant at Niagara, with the reinforcements from the west, reached Irondequoit in the same hour with the division of De Nonville.

After laying waste the country in his course, and taking formal possession of some of the principal villages of the Senecas, De Nonville dispatched a detachment to Fort Frontenac, (Kingston,) to communicate the result of the expedition, and with the rest of his force, set out for Niagara on the 26th, which he reached on the 30th. "In three days," says he, "the army had so fortified the post as to put it in a good condition

De Nonville's Expedition—The Tuscaroras.

of defense in case of an assault." A detachment of one hundred men left here, soon fell beneath the combined attacks of disease and the Senecas, and the post was again deserted. De Nonville left Niagara on the 2d of August. La Hontan was ordered to take a detachment of troops, and accompany the Indian allies on their return to the west. Rowing up from the fort to Lewiston, they carried their canoes over the portage on the American side, and launched them again at Schlosser. Scarcely had they pushed their skiffs from the shore, when a "thousand Iroquois" appeared on the river's bank. It was under the terror of such a pursuit that La Hontan, with three or four savages, left the main body to catch a hurried glimpse of that "fearful cataract" which, in his trepidation, he describes as "seven or eight hundred feet high, and half a league broad."

The facts of De Nonville's expedition are woven into W. H. C. Hosmer's beautiful poem of "Yonnondio."

The Tuscaroras.

The Tuscurora reservation is upon a mountain ridge in the town of Lewiston, about nine miles north-east of the Falls. Driven from their original seats in North Carolina by the aggressions of the whites, they migrated to New York in 1712, and became merged in the confederacy of the Iroquois. In the revolutionary war a part of them inclined to the English, and a part remained neutral. "Such portions of the Tuscaroras and Oneidas as had been allies of the English in their flight from the total rout of Gen. Sullivan, embarked

Niagara Frontier in 1812.

in canoes upon Oneida lake, and down the Oswego river, coasting along up Lake Ontario to the British garrison at Fort Niagara. In the spring, a part of them returned, and a part of them took possession of a mile square upon the mountain ridge, given them by the Senecas. The Holland Company afterward donated to them two square miles adjoining their reservation, and in 1804 they purchased of the company 4329 acres; the aggregate of which several tracts is their present possessions."

Niagara Frontier in 1812.

President Madison's proclamation of war threw the whole frontier into consternation. The pioneers, unprotected by a sufficient force, and dreading the treacherous warfare of the British Indians, were ready to abandon their homes to the tender mercies of the enemy. The strong positions of the Americans were Buffalo and Fort Niagara; those of the British were Fort Erie and Fort George, a redoubt opposite Black Rock, a battery at Chippewa, another below the falls, and the defenses on Queenston Heights.

On the 11th of August, Major General Van Rensselaer, of the New York militia, established his headquarters at Lewiston. On the 13th of October, he determined to cross the river at Lewiston and take possession of Queenston Heights. The attempt was successful. Shortly after the occupation, Gen. Brock arrived with a reinforcement of 600 troops, and, in attempting to rally them after their first repulse, was killed. His aid-de-camp, McDonald, fell, likewise, by his side. Meanwhile, the British having received another reinforcement, the undisciplined militia of Van Rensselaer's rear division, as they had not yet crossed the river, preferred to remain where they were, although they were obliged to see their gallant companions suffer a *total defeat*. This was the chief event on this frontier, in the campaign of 1812. On the 27th of May, 1813, Gen. Dearborn captured from the British, Fort George, at Newark, near Niagara, at the mouth of the Niagara river.

After the British had withdrawn their regular force from the frontier, M'Clure, the American general in command of Fort George, wantonly burned the town of Newark, leaving its homeless inhabitants exposed to the inclemency of the season, evacuated the conquered territory, and returned to his own side of the river. But retribution was at hand. The post evacuated by M'Clure was soon occupied by Col. Murray with a force of 500 British soldiers and Indians. Gen. M'Clure, feeling perfectly secure of Fort Niagara, took up his head-quarters at Buffalo. Col. Leonard, equally secure, slept in his own house, three miles above the fort. Thus it was that the force of Murray, crossing the river before day-break, at a point about four miles above the fort, called the Five Mile Meadows, surprised the garrison, and made themselves masters of the post. Indian scouts left the main body, like bloodhounds, to scent up their prey. The whole frontier was a scene of the most intense suffering. Lewiston, Niagara Falls, Black

War on the Niagara Frontier.

Rock, and Buffalo fell an easy prey to the destroyer. All fled who could, *the militia frequently leading the van* "It was a motley throng, flying from the torch and the tomahawk of an invading foe, with hardly the show of a military organization to cover the retreat." Buffalo was burned to the ground on the 30th of December. But the campaign of 1814 was destined to retrieve, as far as possible the fortunes of this. The executive appointed Gen. Brown to the command in this frontier, associating with him Winfield Scott, Gaines, Miller, and others. Then followed a brilliant succession of victories,—the capture of Fort Erie, the battle of Chippewa, the battle of Lundy's Lane, and finally, the greatest of all victories, peace.

THE
QUEEN'S HOTEL

FRONT STREET,

TORONTO, ONTARIO.

THOMAS DICK, Proprietor.

        THOMAS McGAW Manager.

This House, under its present management, is in every department FIRST CLASS, and has during the past year, undergone many improvements, in Additions, Frescoing, new Parlor, and Elegant Furniture. Much of the Furniture and Tapestry was

IMPORTED EXPRESSLY FOR THE QUEENS.

NORTHERN ROUTE.

This route has long been the favorite one with the traveling million, and we doubt not, reader, that you are purposing to enjoy its offered pleasures. Let us, therefore, take the cars at the Falls, and pass along the river's bank to Lewiston; here take steamers for Toronto, thence for Lake Ontario and the St. Lawrence. Nothing of the kind could be more charming than this short railway passage. The distance from the Falls to Lewiston is seven miles. Three miles below the Falls, the road enters, by an excavation, the side of the bank, and the grade continues as far as Lewiston. The train sweeping along this gorge, your admiration is constantly challenged by a panorama of river scenery seldom equaled on the face of the globe. To describe it would take the pen of a Ruskin; to appreciate it, *it must be seen*—or, take Great Western Railway at Suspension Bridge, two miles below the Falls, for Toronto direct, or Erie and Niagara Railroad for Niagara, at the outlet of Niagara River, thence steamer City of Toronto for Toronto.

Two miles below the Falls, and adjacent to the Suspension Bridge, is

Niagara City;

For such is the present name of the beautiful village, formerly called Bellevue, from its *fine view* of the Falls in the distance. Before the Suspension Bridge was constructed here, no village was to be seen. Its

Niagara City— Lewiston.

population is now about 1200, and it is still increasing
though very slowly since 1857. On the bank of the
river, near the bridge, stands a grist-mill, turned by a
wheel placed 280 feet below, with which it communicates
by a shaft. The town contains, also, an immense railroad
depot, and a sufficient number of stores, offices, and
hotels. Among the latter, the massive stone building
at the northern extremity of the place is one of the
finest structures of the kind in this region of country.
The character of Niagara city changes so rapidly in
its youthful growth that any but the most general description of it must fail to be permanently true.

Lewiston.

On the 24th of May, 1798, Surveyor General De Witt
wrote to Mr. Ellicott, of the Holland Land Company,
"to examine where a town could most conveniently be
placed on the Niagara river, where the Inidan title had
been extinguished," and to "furnish a map and survey
thereof." Mr. Ellicott recommended Lewiston as the
place; and surely a prettier, or at the time more eligible
site, could not have been selected. It lies seven miles
below the Falls, nestling at the foot of the mountain
amid a wealth of "living greenness"— the very ideal of
rural loveliness. As the head of navigation on the
lower Niagara, it is a place of considerable importance;
but has been much injured by the construction of the
Erie and Welland canals. It contains, besides a porpor-
tionate number of stores and hotels, churches of all the
various denominations, and an academy of considerable

size. In 1812, it was the head-quarters of Gen. Van Rensselaer, of the New York militia.

Lewiston Suspension Bridge.

Just above Lewiston, the Niagara is spanned by the longest and one of the finest suspension bridges in the world. Its span is one thousand and forty-five feet. It is supported by ten cables — five upon a side — carried over massive towers of cut stone, and secured by anchors sunk into the solid rock six or seven feet. The cables are each composed of 250 strands of number ten wire, 1245 feet in length. The ultimate capacity of the bridge is estimated at eight hundred and thirty-five tons. This bridge is the property of a joint company of Canadians and Americans, and was erected in 1850, under the superintendence of E. W. Serrell, Esq., of Canada East.

Queenston:

A small village opposite Lewiston, containing about 200 inhabitants, three churches — Episcopal, Presbyterian, and Baptist — a telegraph office, and a tannery. The name of this place is associated in history with the gallant defence by the British of the adjacent heights, in the war of 1812. The village is prettily situated, but its importance has been lessened by the same causes which have retarded the growth of Lewiston.

NOTE.—This beautiful bridge in a violent storm was capsized. We understand it is to be repaired.

Brock's Monument,

On Queenston Heights, just above the village of this name, near the spot where the gallant soldier fell, stands a monument to Gen. Brock, beneath which his ashes and those of his aiddecamp, McDonald, repose. The first monument was completed in 1826, and consisted of a plain shaft of freestone, about 126 feet high, and surmounted by an observatory, reached by spiral stairs on the inside. This was blown up by some miscreant, on the night of the 17th of April, 1840. The present structure,—inaugurated Aug. 13th, 1853, amid the enthusiasm of over ten thousand people present— is far more magnificent than the former. Its whole height is one hundred and eighty-five feet. The sub-base is forty feet square and thirty feet high. On this are placed four lions, facing respectively north, south, east, and west. Next is the base of the pedestal, twenty-one feet six inches, square, and ten feet high. Then comes the pedestal, sixteen feet square and ten feet high, bearing a heavy cornice, ornamented with lion heads alternately with wreaths in alto-relievo. From the top of the pedestal to the top of the base of the shaft, the form changes from square to round. The shaft is a fluted column of freestone, seventy-five feet in height, and ten feet in diameter, surmounted by a Corinthian capital, ten feet high, on which is worked in relief a statue of the Goddess of War. Then comes a round dome, nine feet high, which is reached by 250 spiral steps from the base on the inside. The whole

is surmounted by a massive statue of General ISAAC
BROCK.

Fort Niagara

Is built at the mouth of the Niagara river, on the American side. We have already given the history of this post, in treating of the Niagara Frontier. Within the last few years, important repairs have been made around the fort, and the entire wall has been constructed anew. "During the progress of these repairs, many relics of former days were found. The entrances to several underground passages were discovered; but owing to their ruinous state, they were not entered; could this have been done, no doubt many interesting discoveries would have been made." This spot is interesting as historic ground, when associated with the memory of the heroic La Salle, and the gentle and courtly De Nonville, and all the gallant "chiefs and ladies fair" that have graced its frowning walls. The village adjacent to the fort is called Youngstown, from the name of its founder, the late John Young, Esq. Here was fought the battle of the 24th of July, 1759, in which Prideaux, the English general, fell, and after which the French garrison surrendered to Sir William Johnson, who succeeded to the command of the English.

Niagara,

Opposite Youngstown, is one of the oldest towns in Upper Canada, and was at one time the capital of the province. It is on the site of the old town of Newark, burnt by Gen. M'Clure, December 10th, 1813. It is a

Fort George — Fort Mississaga — Toronto.

pleasant town, facing Lake Ontario on one side, and the river on the other. In former days, its importance was much more considerable than at present. Since the completion of the Welland Canal, St. Catharines, being more centrally situated, has absorbed its trade, and detracted very much from its prosperity.

A short distance above the village are seen the ruins of the old *Fort George*, taken by the Americans, under Dearborn, May 29th, 1813, destroyed by M'Clure, December 10th, and has never been rebuilt. A little below the town is *Fort Mississaga*, where a detachment of British soldiers is stationed.

After leaving the Niagara, we shall describe first the Canadian, and then the American, side of Lake Ontario. You can take the Royal Mail Line Steamers at Toronto for Montreal, or Grand Trunk Railway for Kingston or Prescott. Thence we describe all places in their natural order.

Toronto.

Toronto is situated on Toronto Bay, a beautiful sheet of water, four miles in length, by two miles in width. It is disjoined from Lake Ontario, except at its inlet, by a long, sandy beach. The southwest end of this beach, on which the lighthouse stands, is called *Gibralter Point*. "*Toronto* signifies, in the Indian language, *a place of meeting*. In 1793, when surveyed by the elder Boushette, under the orders of Gov. Simcoe, two Massasanga families were the only inhabitants it contained; and the harbor was a resort for

Toronto — Port Hope.

numerous wild-fowl, while its waters produced an abundance of fish."

The early name of Toronto was Little York. The city is distant thirty-six miles from the mouth of the Niagara River, forty miles from Hamilton, 160 miles from Kingston, 333 miles from Montreal, and 413 miles from Quebec, by railroad.

In the last war, it was taken by the Americans, April 27th, 1813, in an assault led on by *Gen. Pike;* but, in the moment of triumph, that gallant officer, with many of his colleagues, was killed by the explosion of the enemy's magazine.

In 1823, Toronto contained but 4,000 inhabitants. In 1834, it was incorporated as a city. It now contains upwards of 60,000 inhabitants, and is, perhaps, the most beautiful and flourishing city in the two provinces. It is the seat of three colleges, and numerous high schools. Among its many fine buildings are the Parliament House, the governor's residence, the colleges, Osgoode Hall, the banks, the custom-house, the lunatic asylum, St. James' Church, (the English cathedral,) and the Romish cathedral.

The hotels are numerous, and well kept. The Rossin House and Queen's Hotel are first class, the American and Revere Hotels are among the next in grade.

Port Hope

Is sixty-five miles from Toronto. It has four churches — Episcopal, Presbyterian, Methodist, and Baptist — branches of the Upper Canada, and Commercial and Montreal banks, three foundries, and a number of factories and mills.

Cobourg,

Containing about 4,000 inhabitants, lies seven miles below Port Hope. The town contains seven churches, two banks, the largest cloth factory in the province, two foundries, etc.

Kingston.

The French commenced building a fort here as early as 1672, which was finished the next year, and named Fort Frontenac. It was held by the French until destroyed by the expedition under Col. Bradstreet, in 1758. In 1762, it fell into the hands of the English, from whom it obtained its present name. Its population is something over 10,000. Its distance from Cobourg is 110 miles. It has thirteen churches, two colleges, market building, and a *magnificent city hall.*

Let us now return, and briefly glance at the places on the American side of Lake Ontario.

Charlottesville,

At the mouth of the Genesee river, seventy-five miles from the mouth of the Niagara, is the port of entry for Rochester. The river is navigable, by steamers, five miles from its mouth, as far as Carthage, whence passengers can take R. R. cars for Rochester, two miles distant.

Oswego — Ogdensburg — Defeat of the English by the French.

Oswego

Is the next port at which the boat touches. We have spoken in another place of the early project of the French to unite Quebec with the Gulf of Mexico by a contiuous line of military posts. To defeat a project from which the English had so much to fear, Gov. Barnet, of New York and New Jersey, built a fort on the present site of Oswego, at his own expense.

On the 11th of August, 1756, the Marquis De Montcalm, commander of the French forces in Canada, invested the fort, and, on the 12th, reduced Col. Mercer, the English commandant, to the necessity of spiking his guns and retreating across the river to *Little Fort*. Montcalm opened a destructive fire upon the English in their new position, during which Col. Mercer was killed; and, on the 14th, the English agreed to capitulate, on condition of their being protected from the merciless fury of the Indians. After the capitulation, in direct violation of its terms, "Montcalm gave twenty of his prisoners to the custody and tortures of the savage allies, as victims for an equal number of Indians that had been killed during the siege."

The French then razed the fortification to the ground, and returned the land to the Onondaga Indians. Three years afterward, the fort was rebuilt by the English, by whom it was held until delivered up to the United States, in 1796. On the 5th of May, 1814, this post was attacked by above two thousand soldiers and sailors of the British service.

Capture of Little Fort by the British — Sackets Harbor.

Col. Mitchell, with his gallant three hundred, defended the place until he was obliged to yield before overpowering numbers, and then retreated in good order, inflicting five times as great a loss upon the enemy as that which he received.

Oswego is a beautiful and flourishing town, the commercial center of a fertile and wealthy part of country, and contains some of the largest flouring mills in the world. Its population is about fifteen thousand. It is the terminus of both a railroad and a canal, connecting it with Syracuse and the New York Central Railway.

Sackets Harbor,

A small town lying on a spacious bay, forty-five miles below Oswego. It was founded in 1799, by a Mr. Sackett, of Jamaica, L. I., from whom it took its name. From its position on Lake Ontario, it is admirably suited to the purposes of a naval station, and was, in fact, the American head-quarters of the Ontario fleet in the last war. It is now the seat of a military post, called "Madison Barracks."

Cape Vincent

Is a pleasant little town, lying at the head of the St. Lawrence, named in honor of one of the pioneer settlers — M. *Vincent* Le Roy De Chaumont. It is said that this place was selected as the retreat of the Emperor Napoleon, in case he should be obliged to seek an asylum in this country. Cape Vincent is connected

The Thousand Islands — Clayton.

by railway with Chaumont, Brownville, Watertown, and Rome.

The Thousand Islands.

About six miles below Kingston these islands begin, and extend as far as Morristown. Notwithstanding their name, their number is in fact nearly *fifteen hundred*. On account of their size, they are not, at first, very numerous. The largest is Grande, or Wolf Island,—about thirty miles in length. They lessen in size, and increase in number, as you approach *Clayton* — a little town on the American side, and the great rafting station of E. G. Merrick, Esq. Van Cleve's Guide says: " This is, also, the residence of the well-known WILLIAM JOHNSON, who figured in the late Canadian rebellion. In consequence of his participation in these troubles, he was obliged to seclude himself from the search instituted for him by troops under the command of the late General Worth. It was during this seclusion that his daughter, 'KATE,' acquired her title of 'Queen of the Thousand Islands,' from her visiting, and carrying him provisions in her canoe." A few miles below Clayton, the river appears covered with floating islands. Smith, in his "Past, Present and Future of Canada," describes these islands thus: "Islands, of all sizes and shapes, are scattered in profusion throughout the waters; some covered with vegetation; others bare and rugged rocks; some, many acres in extent; others, measuring but a few feet; some showing a bare, bald head, a little above the level of the water, while a short distance off, a large island, or rock, crowned with a considerable growth of pine or cedar, will rise abruptly out of the water, to the height, probably, of a hundred feet and more. These islands are mostly of granite or sandstone. The locality appears to have suffered, in some by-gone time, from some great convulsion of nature." Nearly opposite Clayton, on the Canada side, is Gananoqui, a pretty village of about nine hundred inhabitants, founded in 1798, by the late Col. JOEL STONE, at the confluence of the Gananoqui river with the St. Lawrence. Midway between these two last named towns is *Gore Island.* The next large island below this is *Wellesley Island.* Opposite the lower end of this island, on the American side, is the little rock-perched town of Alexandria.

Brockville,

A pleasant town of about three thousand inhabitants, lying at the foot of the Thousand Islands, on the Canada side of the river. It is situated on an elevation of land which rises from the harbor in a succession of ridges. The town was laid out in 1802, and is now a place of no little importance. In the war of 1812, it was captured by the American major, Forsyth, who was, afterward, killed at La Cole.

Morristown

Is on the American side of the river, directly opposite Brockville. It was first settled by emigrants from

Morristown, New Jersey, by whom it was named, in honor of their native place. The river at this point, is two miles and a half wide.

On the American side, twelve miles below Morristown, is

Ogdensburg.

A mission was founded here about the year 1741, by the Abbe François Picquet — the "Apostle of the Iroquois." As a protection to the mission, and, perhaps, for other purposes less sacred, a fort was built at the same time, called "La Presentation." Remains of this fort are said to be visible at the present day. The corner-stone has been dug up, and is now in the possession of an inhabitant of the town. It bears the following inscription:

In nomine † Dei Omnipotentis
Huic habitationi initio dedit,
Frans Picquet, 1749.

Ogdensburg was twice attacked by the British, during the last war — once in 1812, but without success, and again in 1813, when it was captured, plundered, and a portion of it burnt. On the arrival of the boats, the cars leave Ogdensburg for Rouse's Point, on Lake Champlain — one hundred and eighteen miles distant — where they connect with trains to Boston and Montreal.

Prescott — Fort Wellington — Windmill Point — The Rapids.

Prescott

Is an old-fashioned looking town, of about two thousand inhabitants, on the Canada side, opposite Ogdensburg. Before the opening of the Rideau canal, Prescott was the center of the carrying trade between Kingston and Montreal; but since that event its growth has been checked. The place has several factories and mills, five churches, and is a port of entry. On the eastern side of the town, a fortification has been thrown up, called *Fort Wellington*. About a mile below the town is a place called *Windmill Point* — a collection of stone buildings, in which the "Patriots established themselves in 1837, under one *Von Shultz*, a Polish exile, and held out against the British troops for three days.

About five miles below Ogdensburg, *the first rapid of the St. Lawrence* breaks around an islet called *Chimney Island*, from a number of old stones that have remained standing from some early fortification.

The next town on the American side is *Waddington* — and in the river, over against it, *Ogden Island*, from the name of its proprietor. On the Canada side is *Morrisburg*, formerly called *West Williamsburg*. It contains about two hundred inhabitants, and is called the port of *Mariatown*, although the settlement bearing that name is two miles distant. A short distance below Morristown is *Chryseler's Farm*, where an American force was met, on its descent to Montreal, in 1813, and defeated and turned back, by a detachment of the British troops. Thirty miles below Ogdensburg, the

Long Sault Rapid — Cornwall — St. Regis.

boat touches at *Louisville*, whence stages run to *Massena Springs*—distant seven miles. These springs are said to have proved effectual in restoring debilitated constitutions.

The Long Sault,

A continuous rapid for over nine miles, divided in the center by Long Sault Island. The channel on the north side of the island is called "*Lost Channel*," from a once prevalent belief that any thing so luckless as to be drawn into it must inevitably be lost. It is now descended with safety, although the usual path of steamers is on the south side.

Cornwall

Is situated at the foot of the Long Sault, on the Canada side. It is "a neat, quiet, old-fashioned looking town," of about sixteen hundred inhabitants, but not a place of much business. Cornwall Island lies in the river, opposite the town, and belongs to the Indians of

St. Regis.

This is an old Indian village, a little way below Cornwall, on the opposite side of the river. The tourist will observe, from the deck of the steamer, the old church, lifting its tin roof above the neighboring houses. The bell hanging in this church is associated with a deed of genuine Indian revenge. On its way from France. it was captured by an English cruiser, and taken into Salem, Massachusetts, where it was sold to the church at Deerfield, in the same state. The Indians, hearing of the destination of their bell, set out for Deerfield, attacked the town, killed forty-seven of the inhabitants, and took one hundred and twelve captives, "among whom was the pastor and his family." The bell was then taken down, and conveyed to St. Regis, where it now hangs.

Lake St. Francis.

This is the name of that expansion of the St. Lawrence which begins just below Cornwall and St. Regis and extends to *Coteau du Lac*. Many little islands are scattered here and there over its surface. *Coteau du Lac* is a small village at the foot of the lake; and, on the north side, over against this place, is *Grand Island*. Just below are the *Coteau Rapids*. *The Cedars* is a small town just above the rapids of this name. Passing these rapids — a very exciting passage — you glide into Lake St. Louis, from which you catch a view of Montreal mountain in the distance. On the right you see Nun's Island, belonging to the *Grey Nunnery*, at Montreal. Passing out from Lake St. Louis, the first place we reach after having left the lake is *La Chine* — a town nine miles distant from Montreal, and connected with it by railroad. Below the town, the *La Chine Rapids* begin — a current so swift and wild that, to avoid it, the *La Chine Canal* has been cut around it. After passing these rapids, we glide past the little village of *La Prairie*, and are in full view of beetling heights and the city of

Montreal — Black Nunnery — Grey Nunnery.

Montreal.

At the dawn of Canadian history, the site of this place was occupied by an Indian village, called Hochelaga. Subsequently becoming a French trading-station, and, still later, the political center of the colonial government, it advanced quickly into prosperity and importance. Its growth, however, was not unattended by those savage cruelties so fatally incident to the early settlements on this continent. In the summer of 1668, a party of Iroquois Indians — the hereditary enemies of the French — stealthily landed their canoes on the island, and cruelly massacred men, women, and children, to the number of over one thousand. Again peopled, it continued, for a long time, the head-quarters of the French forces in Canada; and its fall, in 1759, was the virtual announcement of the conquest of the country. At the peace of 1763, it was surrendered to the English; and, in 1775, was taken, and temporarily occupied by the Americans, under General MONTGOMERY. Although so long under English rule, Montreal is still a *French city*. One of the most obvious notes of the visitor is, that the city is divided, by its *styles*, into an old part and a new — the long narrow streets, darkened by high, steep-roofed houses, plainly indicating the former. Among the principal objects of curiosity in the city are the cathedral, an imposing structure of granite, capable of holding fifteen thousand persons; the "Black Nunnery," not open to visitors; the "Grey Nunnery," open to visitors; the monument to Lord

Nelson, on Notre Dame street; the quays of the city, the finest on this continent; and, to many, the mountain itself, against which the city is built. A Macadamized road has been laid around this mountain, and the drive over it is far from unpleasant.

On that part of the island opposite the mouth of the Ottawa river stood a chapel, in early times, dedicated to Saint Ann. To the fur traders' custom of stopping at this place, and imploring the protection of the tutelar saint, before ascending the Ottawa on their long trading expeditions, Moore gracefully alludes in his Canadian Boat Song.

> "Faintly as tolls the evening chime,
> Our voices keep tune, and our oars keep time.
> Soon as the woods on shore look dim,
> We'll sing at St. Ann's our parting hymn.

If you prefer to continue directly on from Montreal, you take the Grand Trunk Railroad cars for *Rouse's Point*. This latter place, situated at the north-western extremity of Lake Champlain, is likewise the terminus of the Ogdensburg Railroad; and here passengers for Saratoga, or any of the intermediate points, take the Champlain boats. Passengers for Boston can either take the Vermont Central Railroad here, or if they prefer a sail as far as Burlington, can there take the Burlington and Rutland Railroad, or from Montreal, continue by the Grand Trunk Railsoad to White Mountains, Boston. &c.

Lake Champlain — Burlington — Crown Point — Ticonderoga.

Lake Champlain.

Samuel Champlain, at the head of a company of Rouen merchants, established himself at Quebec, in 1603, and having soon afterward espoused the cause of the Hurons against the Iroquois, joined an expedition against the latter in 1608. On this expedition, he discovered the beautiful lake which still bears his name. The length of the lake is one hundred and twenty miles. It contains several islands — the two largest of which are situated toward its northern extremity, and are called, respectively, *North Hero* and *South Hero*. The places on the route are, Plattsburg, on the western side of the lake — the scene of Commodore McDonough's brilliant victory over the invading force of Prevost, September 11, 1814; Burlington, on the east side of the lake — beautifully situated on a slope which rises gently from the water toward a distant girdle of hills, near which place repose the remains of Col. Ethan Allen; Crown Point, on the west side of the lake — the old Fort St. Frederic of the French — built by the French in 1731, captured by the English in 1759, and taken from the latter by the Americans under Col. Warner in 1775 — is now in ruins; Ticonderoga (from Cheonderoga, its Indian name,) is situated on a tongue of land between Lake Champlain and the outlet of Lake St. George. This place was built by the French in 1756, it was taken by the English in 1759, and from them captured by Ethan Allen, on the 10th of May, 1775, — the same day that Crown

Surrender of Fort Ticonderoga to Allen.

Point surrendered to Colonel Warner. "The commandant of the fort was surprised in his bed by Allen, Arnold, and a few of their followers, who had entered by a subterranean passage, and made themselves masters of it without any loss. On being asked to surrender, he asked by what authority he was required to do so. Allen replied, 'I demand it in the name of the great Jehovah, and of the Continental Congress.'"

The Champlain boats pass up the lake to Whitehall; but many prefer taking carriages at Ticonderoga for the *Lake George Steamboat Landing*, distant three miles and a half, and there taking the *Lake George* boat for Caldwell, at the southern limit of the lake.

Lake George is thirty-three miles in length. Its Indian name was *Horicon*. By the French it was called *Lac Sacrement*, from the *purity* of its waters. At Caldwell, passengers take the stages to *Moreau Station*, and the cars from there to *Saratoga*.

At Caldwell is the ruins of Fort William Henry, the site of which is now occupied by the commodious and elegant Fort William Henry Hotel.

FROM MONTREAL
TO
OTTAWA CITY & UPPER OTTAWA.

Tourists leaving Montreal for the Ottawa may proceed by either one of the following routes: (1) **By steamer**, directly from the city; (2) by the **Grand Trunk Railway** to St. Annes, a distance of 21 miles, and thence, by steamer, up the river; (3) by railroad to Prescott, 113 miles, thence, by the Ottawa and Prescott Railroad, to Ottawa city; (4) by railroad to *La Chine*, 9 miles, and there take the steamer for Ottawa city. After leaving Montreal, the following places are passed:

St. Anne's,

A small village deriving its name from the chapel alluded to above, is situated on the south-western end of the island of Montreal. The river is here broken into rapids, and dotted with several small islands. At this place, also, the steamer passes through a lock, 45 feet in width, and 180 feet in length.

Lake of the Two Mountains.

About two miles west of St. Anne's, the Ottawa expands into a lake bearing this name. The width of this lake is about eight, and its length about ten,

Indian Village of Two Mountains — Carillon — Point Fortune.

miles. It derives its name from two mountains just to the north, which tower up to an elevation of over 400 feet each.

The Indian Village of the Two Mountains

Lies on the northern bank of the Ottawa, about 25 miles from *La Chine*. The remnants of two once mighty tribes—the Mohawks and the Algonquins—reside at this place. The river here contracts, and, for about a mile, continues contracted to the width of but a half a mile; afterward, it again expands into the *Upper Lake of the Two Mountains*. Nine miles further on, it resumes its narrowest limit.

Carillon,

Eight miles above the Indian village, and on the same side of the river. The ascent of the river, here interrupted by the rapids, is continued, for twelve miles, by means of a lock and canal.

Point Fortune,

Opposite Carillon. Tourists for the *Caledonia Springs* here leave the steamer, and proceed by stage.

Greenville,

Twelve miles above Carillon. Boats here leave the canal, and reënter the Ottawa.

GUIDE TO THE OTTAWA. 93

Rideau Falls — Chaudiere Falls — Ottawa city.

Rideau Falls,

A short distance below the city of Ottawa. The Rideau river here precipitates itself into the Ottawa over a ledge of rock thirty feet in height, forming one of the most attractive features of the Ottawa scenery.

Chaudiere Falls,

(The Boiling Pot.) "Six miles above the Ottawa, begin the rapids terminating in the Ottawa *Chaudiere Falls*, which, inferior in impressive grandeur to the Falls of *Niagara*, are, perhaps, more permanently interesting, as presenting greater variety. The greatest height of Chaudiere Falls is about forty feet. Arrayed in every imaginable variety of form—in vast, dark masses, in graceful cascades, or in tumbling spray—they have been well described as a hundred rivers struggling for a passage. Not the least interesting feature which they present is the *Lost Chaudiere*, where a body of water, greater in volume than the Thames at London, is quietly sucked down, and disappears underground."

Ottawa City.

[We take the liberty of extracting the following description of this place from the *Canadian Tourist*.]

The city of *Ottawa* is, perhaps, situated more picturesquely than any other in North America, with the exception of Quebec. The view from the *Barrack Hill* — embracing, as it does, in one *coup d'œil*, the magnificent *Falls* of the *Chaudiere*, with its clouds of snowy spray, generally spanned by a brilliant rainbow; the suspension bridge, uniting Upper and Lower Canada; the river above the great falls, studded with pretty, wooded islands; and the distant, purple mountains, which divide the waters of the Gatineau from those of the Ottawa — is one of the most beautiful in the world.

The city, now containing about fourteen thousand inhabitants, sprung up, about forty years ago, from a collection of shanties inhabited by the laborers and artificers employed by the Royal Engineers to construct the *Rideau Canal*. This canal, terminating at Kingston, was intended by the government of England to be a means of communication between the lower St. Lawrence and the Lakes, in case the communication on the first should be interrupted. The Canal was designed by Colonel By, of the Royal Engineers, and the present city of Ottawa was named *Bytown*, in memory of its founder, until, a few years ago, the inhabitants petitioned the Provincial Parliament to change its name.

The canal is a splendid specimen of engineering skill; and the masonry of the numerous locks is generally admired for its finish and solidity. Eight of these locks rise, one above another, directly in the center of the city, the canal being crossed by a handsome stone bridge just above them. The canal, in

Ottawa city.

fact, divides the city into two parts—the upper town and the lower town.

During the summer months, steamers run daily between Ottawa and Montreal, and between Ottawa and Kingston, by way of the Rideau Canal. Two trains leave the city every day for *Prescott*, where those passengers who intend to go to Montreal change into the cars of the Grand Trunk line, and so reach Montreal by railway.

Travelers who wish to proceed farther up the river, can take a carriage, or omnibus, for Aylmer, a pretty village about nine miles from Ottawa, where they will find a steamer which takes them to *Chatts;* from this, there is a railway about two miles; they then proceed by another steamer to *Portage du Fort*, (60 miles above Ottawa;) here wagons are used for a short distance, and another steamer takes them to *Pembroke*, (100 miles above Ottawa,) and still another from that point to *Deux Joachim;* where, for the present, navigation ceases for any thing larger than a canoe. A railroad is under construction from Pembroke to Brockville.

Ottawa City is the Capital of the Dominion of Canada. The Parliament buildings are magnificent structures built in the most substantial manner, and in the latest style of architecture.

COHEN & LOPEZ,

IMPORTERS OF
Fine Havana

INCLUDING

"PARTAGAS,"   "ESPANOLO,"
"FIGARO,"   "CABANAS,"
"UPMANN,"   AND OTHER
"LA ROSA DE   CHOICE
SANTIOGA,"   BRANDS.

THE FINEST ASSORTMENT OF
TOBACCONISTS' GOODS IN CANADA
Will be found at this Establishment.

CORNER PLACE D'ARMES & ST. JAMES STREET
Near the Bank of Montreal,

Montreal.

FROM

MONTREAL TO QUEBEC.

The tourist will choose his route to Quebec, either by the Grand Trunk Railway, or — if in the season of navigation — by steamer down the St. Lawrence. If he choose the latter, he will pass:

The Island of St. Helen,

Midway across the river, and opposite the lower part of the city of Montreal. Just below this island, the river is broken by a small rapid, called St. Mary's.

Longueuil,

Three miles below the city, on the south bank of the river — the present terminus of the St. Lawrence and Atlantic Railway.

Sorel, or William Henry,

Forty-five miles below Montreal, at the junction of the Richlieu with the St. Lawrence — a pleasant town, with a population of about 3000, and the first stopping-place for steamers on their way to Quebec.

Lake St. Peter's

An expanse of the St. Lawrence, beginning at a point about five miles below *Sorel*, and continuing for twenty-five miles. The greatest width of this lake is nine miles. On its southern shore is *Point St. Francis*, eighty-two miles from *Montreal*.

Three Rivers,

One of the oldest towns in Canada (founded in 1618,) with a population of about six thousand — is situated at the confluence of the St. Maurice and St. Lawrence rivers, midway between Montreal and Quebec, and ninety miles from either.

Batiscau,

On the north side of the river, 63 miles above Quebec. It is the last stopping-place for steamers before reaching Quebec.

Quebec

Is situated on the confluence of the St. Lawrence and the St. Charles, 180 miles below Montreal, and 400 miles above the gulf. "The city is built on the extremity of a ridge terminating in the angle formed by the junction of the two rivers, on the point called Cape Diamond, which here rises to the height of about 340 feet above the St. Lawrence. The cape is surmounted by the citadel, and the city extends from it, principally in a N. E. direction, down to the water's edge. The old town which lies wholly without the walls, partly at the foot of cape Diamond, and around to the St. Charles, has narrow, and, in parts, steep streets. The ascent from the upper to the lower portion of the city, which crosses, the line of the fortifications, is by a winding

Quebec.

street, and a flight of steps. The public buildings and most of the houses are built of stone. There are 174 streets in the city and suburbs, the principal of which are the following: St. John Street, the principal seat of the retail trade; St. Louis Street, occupied by lawyers' offices and private dwellings, is handsome and well built; D'Aautervil Street, facing the Esplanade in the upper town; and, in the lower town, St. Peter Street, in which most of the banks, insurance companies, and merchants' offices are situated.

"The Roman Catholic Cathedral is a large and commodious building, but with no pretensions to beauty of architecture; the interior is handsomely fitted up, and and has several fine paintings. The church will seat four thousand persons. It has a fine choir, and a good organ. The Episcopal Cathedral is a handsome edifice, 135 feet by 75 feet. It was erected in 1804, and will seat between three thousand and four thousand persons. Prominent among the other public buildings are the Court House and City Hall, the Marine Hospital, the Lunatic Asylum, the Quebec Musical Hall, the three nunneries, and the Quebec Exchange."

"The situation of Quebec is highly advantageous, in a commercial as well as a military point of view; and its appearance is very imposing, from whatever quarter it is first approached. Though at a distance of 400 miles from the sea, the magnificent river on which it is seated is three miles in breadth a little below the town, and narrows into about a mile in breadth imme-

Quebec.

ately abreast of the citadel, having, in both these parts, sufficient depth of water for the largest ships in the world — a rise and fall of twenty feet in its tides — and space enough in its capacious basin, between Cape Diamond, on the one hand, and the Isle of Orleans, on the other, to afford room and anchorage for a thousand sail of vessels at a time, sheltered from all winds, and perfectly secure."— BUCKINGHAM'S *Canada*.

VICINITY OF QUEBEC.

Falls of Montmorenci,

EIGHT miles below the city of Quebec, should not fail to be visited by all. The height of the fall is 250 feet, 40 feet higher than that of Niagara, but the width of the river at this point is but 50 feet.

"The effect of the view of these falls, on the beholder," says Prof. Silliman, "is most delightful. The river, at some distance, seems suspended in the air, in a sheet of billowy foam; and, contrasted, as it is, with the black, frowning abyss into which it falls, it is an object of the highest interest. The sheet of foam which first breaks over the ridge is more and more divided, as it plunges and is dashed against the successive layers of rock, which it almost completely vails from view. The spray becomes very delicate and abundant from top to bottom, hanging over, and revolving around, the torrents, till it becomes lighter and more evanescent than the whitest fleecy clouds of summer, than the finest attenuated web, than the lightest gossamer, constituting the most airy and sumptuous drapery that can be imagined. Yet, like the drapery of some of the Grecian statues, which, while it vails, exhibits more forcibly the form beneath, this does not hide, but exalts, the effects produced by this noble cataract."

Chaudiere Falls,

Nine miles below Quebec the river *Chaudiere* leaps into the St. Lawrence over a precipice 130 feet in height. The width of the fall is about 400 feet.

The Island of Orleans

Lies in the St. Lawrence, just below Quebec. It is nineteen miles in length by five and a half miles in width, and has a population of about 6000.

Falls of St. Anne,

At the confluence of the river St. Anne with the St. Lawrence, 24 miles below Quebec. The surrounding scenery is both wild and beautiful.

Lake St. Charles,

Thirteen miles north of Quebec, is celebrated for its fine trout, and hence a beautiful resort for anglers.

River Saguenay.

This river falls into the St. Lawrence at the distance of one hundred and forty miles below the city of Quebec. From its source in Lake St. John to its outlet in the St. Lawrence it has a length of one hundred and twenty six miles. It is navigable for the largest vessels to a point about sixty miles from its mouth. "The passage of the waters of the Saguenay from below Ha Ha Bay to the St. Lawrence — a distance of fifty miles — is one of the wonders of nature. They penetrate through a mountainous tract, composed of

River Saguenay — Eternity Point — White Mountains.

sienite granite, forming an immense canal in many places, with banks of perpendicular rocks rising from a thousand to fifteen hundred feet above the surface of the river, which is from a hundred to a hundred and fifty fathoms deep nearly the whole way, and from a mile to three miles broad."

The country of Saguenay is but very sparsely inhabited. At Ha Ha Bay there is a church, and about 150 families; and settlements are beginning at various other places on the river.

Eternity Point and Cape Trinity.

At the distance of 34 miles from the mouth of the Saguenay, two immense masses of rocks rise abruptly from the water's edge to an elevation of 1500 feet. These are called Eternity Point and Cape Trinity. Gazing from the deck of the steamer to the "skyey pinnacles" of these blasted crags, the mind is filled with emotions of indescribable sublimity.

The White Mountains.

From Montreal or Quebec to Portland, Boston, or New York, through the White Mountains.—Every tourist will, of course, visit the "Switzerland of America," if possible. Perhaps there is nothing grander in mountain scenery than the White Mountains of New Hampshire. The station at which visitors usually stop is Gorham, where they find an elegant and comfortable resting place in the Alpine House. Thence, they proceed by carriages, eight miles, to the Glen House, and there take saddle-horses for the ascent of Mt. Washington. The Grand Trunk Railway, starting from Montreal or Quebec, runs directly in view of the Notch, affording the tourist an opportunity of stopping at choice, an hour or a month, in the midst of a scene of unrivaled sublimity, and then proceeding with almost lightning speed to the bustling marts of the east.

New York and Boston are thus brought within a few hours' distance of the White Mountains, and bring out, by contrast, the remembered sublimity into the vividness of an immediate impression.

The White Mountains are situated in Coos County, N. H., and consist of a number of mountain peaks from four to six thousand feet in altitude, the highest of them being Mount Washington, which is six thousand, two hundred and forty-three feet above the level of the sea, and possesses the greatest attraction to tourists. Its ascent has lately become quite fashionable with visitors to the Mountains. The "Notch" is a narrow gorge between two enormous cliffs, and extends for a distance of two miles. Its entrance is about twenty feet wide, and the mountain scenery, diversified by beautiful cascades falling over perpendicular rocks, is grand in the extreme. The *Willey House* stands in this notch, at an elevation of two thousand feet. It is pointed out to the traveler as the residence of the Willey family who perished by an avalanche from the mountain forty years ago. In Franconia Notch may be seen the Basin and Flume,

The White Mountains.

objects of great interest. The Flume is a stream of water having a fall of two hundred and fifty feet over fearful precipices into a natural cavity in the rocks, which forms the basin. The "Old Man of the Mountain," or Profile Mountain, is a singularly interesting natural object. It obtains its name from the striking resemblance it bears to the profile of the human countenance, every feature being marked with the greatest accuracy. Tourists will find a number of excellent hotels at the various mountains — the Alpine House, the Glen House, the Willey House, Crawford's, Gibbs, Fayban's, and others.

TIFFT HOUSE,
BUFFALO, N. Y.

HODGES, Proprietor.

(Late of American Hotel.)

NEW AND ELEGANT
IN EVERY DEPARTMENT.

R. W. COWAN,
Fashionable
First Prize Hatter and Furrier,
No. 416 NOTRE DAME ST.
Corner of St. Peter Street,   *MONTREAL.*

Five First Prizes Eastern Exhibition, Montreal, 1870.
Five First Prizes Western Exhibition, Toronto, 1870.

Eastern Railroad

OF MASSACHUSETTS.

J. B. BAKER, Treas., Boston, Mass.   C. P. HATCH, Gen'l Manager.

RUNNING BETWEEN

BOSTON & PORTLAND.

This popular THROUGH ROUTE between PORTLAND and BOSTON, are running

SEVEN THROUGH PASSENGER TRAINS DAILY

To AND FROM BOSTON AND PORTLAND,

And Connecting with all trains

East and West, North and South.

Through Passenger Trains leave Boston 7:30 A. M., 8:30 A. M., 12:15 P. M., 3:00 P. M., 4:45 P. M., 6:00 P. M and 8:00 P M, for the following places and their connections:

Somerville,
S. Malden,
Chelsea River,
W. Lynn,
Lynn,
Swampscott,
Salem,
Beverly,
N. Beverly,
Wenham,

Ipswich,
Rawley,
Newberryport,
Salisbury,
Seabrook,
Hampton Falls,
Hampton,
N. Hampton,
Greenland,
Portsmouth,

Portland.

Trains leave Portland for Boston and intermediate places and their connections, 6:00, 8:40 and 10,45 A. M., 2:00, 7:45, 8:30 and 10:0 P. M.

At Portland Trains connect with Grand Trunk Railroad for White Mountains, Montreal, Quebec, Saguenay, and all places West and North; with Vermont Central for White Mountains, Lake Champlain, etc.

At Boston, the Eastern Railroad connects with all Railroads in New England, also Railroads and Steamers to New York.

1872.   To Tourists and Travelers.   1872.

NEW AND IMPORTANT ARRANGEMENT.

Grand Trunk R. W.
—AND—
Canadian Inland Steam
Navigation Line of Through Steamers.

NIAGARA FALLS TO MONTREAL,
Quebec, Riviere du Loup, White Mountains, Portland, Boston, Lake George, Saratoga, New York, the River Saguenay.

This Line, now comprising the original Royal Mail and American lines, is composed of Twelve First Class Steamers, and is the only line affording Passengers an opportunity of viewing the unrivalled scenery of the Thousand Islands and the Rapids of the River St. Lawrence.

This route possesses peculiar advantages, as by it parties have their choice of conveyance between Niagara Falls and Quebec over the whole or any portion of it, consequently should the weather prove unfavorable, Passengers may avoid Lake Ontario by taking the Grand Trunk Road to Kingston or Prescott, and from thence by one of the above Steamers, making close connections. No extra charge for meals.

☞ The Only Route to the White Mountains by which parties can ascend the far-famed Mount Washington by the Carriage Road.

☞ American Money taken at par for Tickets by this line, which can be obtained at most of the principal Cities of the United States. Arrangements have also been made with the proprietors of the Principal Hotels at Toronto, Montreal and Quebec, to take American Money at par, charging New York Hotel Rates.

ALEX MILLOY, Gen Agent C. I. S N. Co.,..........Montreal.
H. SHACKELL, Gen Pass Agent G. T R,............Montreal.
C. J BRYDGES, Man'g Director G. T. R,..........Montreal.

E. BARBER, Joint Agent, Niagara Falls.

W. E. TUN

——WHOLESALE——

tationer,

ookseller,

ewsdealer

ALL KINDS OF

Railroad, Law and Mercantile

PRINTING AND BINDING

Done on Shortest Possible Notice.

PRICES LOW.   QUALITY GUARANTEED.

---

80 Woodward Avenue, Detroit, Mich.

G. W. R. R. Buildings, Hamilton, Ont.

3h & Co,

SUCCESSORS TO

J. G. JOSEPH & CO'S RETAIL,

KING STREET,

Established 1838.   **TORONTO.**

JEWELLERS

MANUFACTURING GOLD AND SILVERSMITHS

IMPORTERS OF

Fine Gold and Silver Watches

EUROPEAN AND AMERICAN SILVER PLATE, CLOCKS,
BRONZES, AND FANCY ARTICLES,
Suitable for Presentation,

CRICKETING, OUT AND IN-DOOR GAMES,

Masonic Jewels and Regalia

LONDON AND PARIS HOUSE   KING STREET EAST

www.ingramcontent.com/pod-product-compliance
Lightning Source LLC
Chambersburg PA
CBHW030357170426
43202CB00010B/1408